THE NEW YORK
PUBLIC LIBRARY
AMAZING
MYTHOLOGY

A Book of Answers for Kids

THE NEW YORK PUBLIC LIBRARY AMAZING MYTHOLOGY
A Book of Answers for Kids

Brendan January

A Stonesong Press Book

John Wiley & Sons, Inc.
New York • Chichester • Weinheim • Brisbane • Singapore • Toronto

This book is printed on acid-free paper. ⊗

Copyright ©2000 by The New York Public Library and The Stonesong Press, Inc.

All rights reserved
Published by John Wiley & Sons, Inc.
Published simultaneously in Canada.

The name "The New York Public Library" and the representation of the lion appearing in this work are trademarks and the property of The New York Public Library, Astor, Lenox, and Tilden Foundations.

This publication is designed to provide accurate and authoritative information in regard to the subject matter covered. It is sold with the understanding that the publisher is not engaged in rendering legal, accounting, or other professional services. If legal advice or other expert assistance is required, the services of a competent professional person should be sought.

Library of Congress Cataloging-in-Publication Data

January, Brendan.
    The New York Public Library amazing mythology: a book of answers for kids / Brendan January.
        p. cm.
    Includes bibliographical references.
    Summary: Over 200 questions and answers introduce myths from many ancient cultures, including Egyptian, Greek, Roman, Celtic, Norse, and Native American.
    ISBN 0-471-33205-4 (paper)
    1. Mythology Miscellanea Juvenile literature. [1. Mythology Miscellanea 2. Questions and answers.] I. Title. II. Title: Amazing Mythology.

BL311.J36   2000   99-32203
291.1′3—dc21

Printed in the United States of America

10 9 8 7 6 5 4 3 2 1

CONTENTS

INTRODUCTION

Throughout history, men and women have searched for meaning in the world around them. They wondered why the summer brought blasts of heat and the winter brought chills. They tried to understand the terrifying roar of thunder and the destructive flash of lightning. They attempted to protect themselves against mysterious diseases and famines. Today, we use science to explain how and why these events happen. In the ancient world, people told stories. These stories are now known as myths.

Myths were critically important to past societies. In addition to explaining the forces of nature, myths taught people how to worship the gods and win their favor. Others explained the origins of a city's laws or religious festivals. Often, myths were spoken aloud or acted out to entertain crowds of people, just like we watch movies today.

The word myth *comes from the Greek word* mythos, *meaning saying or story.*

Members of almost every culture in the world told myths. Usually, they were spoken aloud at ceremonies and festivals. Myths were passed down orally from one generation to the next for thousands of years.

With the development of writing, ancient authors wrote down myths and grouped them together into collections or sagas. Other myth tellers were expert craftspeople, and they carved the stories and characters of myths into stone or painted them onto pots. Many stories survived as artifacts that were later recovered by archaeologists and pieced together to tell the ancient mythologies as we know them today.

Several common themes appear in the world's mythologies. Almost every society developed stories to explain how the world and people came into existence. These stories are called creation myths.

Another group of myths explained why men and women suffer from pain and misfortune and why people die. A good example is the Greek myth of Pandora, who disobeyed the gods and opened a box—Pandora's Box—releasing sorrow and disease into the world.

People around the world also told stories about the destructive forces of nature. Mesopotamian, Greek, Chinese, and American Indian mythologies tell of a giant flood that covered the earth, killing people and animals.

All cultures love to hear stories about heroes and cunning characters called tricksters. These individuals changed their world and inspire us with their courage and resourcefulness. Many mythologies tell how a brave person or animal stole fire from the gods and gave it to humankind, thus providing people with an essential tool for civilization.

This book uses questions and answers to tell myths from around the world. Unfortunately, not all myths and traditions could be included. If you want to know more about a particular myth or mythology in general, visit the New York Public Library or your local library and check out the books listed in the bibliography and the recommended reading list at the end of this book.

A Note on the Use of Names

This book discusses a wide variety of cultures and civilizations. Some of these civilizations shared myths and deities with each other or inherited and adapted old myths and deities into later cultures. For this reason, the same deity is often known by two different names in two different cultures. In addition, some languages do not use the Roman alphabet that English uses, and translating names into English has resulted in different spellings.

In this book, the names of deities are spelled as they are most commonly seen in English. Often, especially in the case of Greek and Roman gods, the spelling of the name the deity was first known by is used—for example, the Hercules of the Romans was originally the Herakles of the Greeks.

MIDDLE EASTERN AND AFRICAN CULTURES

MESOPOTAMIA

The word
Mesopotamia
*means land
between two
rivers.*

Where was Mesopotamia?

Mesopotamia existed between two mighty rivers, the Tigris and the Euphrates, in the part of the world we now call the Middle East. This region is called the "cradle of civilization" because it was one of the first places in which humans farmed, raised animals, developed a written language, and created a calendar.

What is the Mesopotamian myth of creation?

The Mesopotamians believed that the universe began as water. The water was ruled over by the god, Apsu, and the goddess, Tiamat. Apsu and Tiamat had several children and grandchildren who often quarreled loudly among themselves, sometimes violently. Desperate for some peace, Apsu decided to destroy them all. The god Ea learned of the plan and decided to strike first. Using trickery, he killed Apsu. Ea and his wife, Damkina, celebrated their victory by building a beautiful cottage, where Damkina gave birth to a son, called Marduk.

Who was Marduk?

Marduk was a powerful prince who had four ears, four eyes, and breathed fire from his throat. He was also full of

This glazed brick relief of one of the dragons of Marduk was created around 600 B.C. as part of the Ishtar Gate of Babylon, a ceremonial entrance for the king during the New Year's Festival. Babylon is in Mesopotamia.

pride, and the other gods grew so angry at his boasts that they asked Tiamat to destroy him. Pleased by the chance to avenge Apsu's death, Tiamat created an army of hideous monsters and gods.

Leading her army, Tiamat attacked Ea, who was so terrified by the horde of monsters that he turned and fled. The other gods saw Ea's defeat and began to fear for their own lives. Desperate, they asked Marduk to defend them. Marduk agreed, but only if they crowned him leader of the gods. Having little choice, the gods made Marduk supreme leader.

With hurricane winds and lightning at his command, Marduk rode into battle in a chariot drawn by four dragons. Hissing with fury, Tiamat lunged at Marduk, but Marduk cast a net and snared her. While Tiamat strained to escape, Marduk fired an arrow into her open mouth and down her throat, killing her. Marduk then turned on Tiamat's army, killing Tiamat's general, Kingu, and capturing the other monsters in a net and throwing them into the underworld.

How did Marduk create the universe and its people?

With Tiamat dead and her army destroyed, Marduk lifted his sword and split her massive skull in two. With one piece, Marduk made the earth; with the other piece, he fashioned the heavens. He created the moon, the sun, and set the stars in the night sky. Marduk then decided to create servants for the gods—people. Using the flesh and bones of Kingu, Marduk molded the first men and women and gave them life.

Who were Gilgamesh and Enkidu?

Gilgamesh was a Mesopotamian king famous for his courage and skill in battle. But he was also a hard ruler who demanded absolute obedience from his subjects. Weary of his harsh rule, Gilgamesh's people prayed to the goddess Aruru to create a monster to defeat Gilgamesh in combat.

In response to the prayers, Aruru created Enkidu, a fierce and hairy god who lived in the countryside like an animal. Enkidu and Gilgamesh clashed in a violent wrestling match that lasted for hours. Finally, the exhausted Gilgamesh was forced to surrender. But the two warriors did not stay enemies. Enkidu was impressed by Gilgamesh's strength, and Gilgamesh admired the opponent who had finally defeated him. Each full of respect for the other, Gilgamesh and Enkidu became fast friends. Gilgamesh invited Enkidu to live in his palace, and together they hunted and battled monsters.

Once Ishtar, goddess of love and war, tried to seduce Gilgamesh, but he spurned her advances. Stung by Gilgamesh's rejection, Ishtar sent a beast called the Bull of Heaven to destroy Gilgamesh's city and people. Enkidu attacked the bull, plunging his sword into its back and tearing out its heart. Furious that her bull was defeated, Ishtar cursed Enkidu and struck him down with a deadly disease. Gilgamesh bitterly mourned his friend's death and resolved that neither he, nor any of his people, would ever die.

Where did Gilgamesh search for eternal life?

Gilgamesh sought a man named Utnapishtim, who lived on a remote island and enjoyed eternal life. The journey was long and dangerous. Along the way, Gilgamesh arrived in the garden of a goddess, who

This colossal stone relief of the hero Gilgamesh was created by Assyrian artists between 1500 and 600 B.C. The Assyrian kingdom and its gods were later absorbed by the Babylonian empire.

advised him to accept death and return to his home. But Gilgamesh refused, and the goddess directed him to the boat that took him to Utnapishtim's island.

Gilgamesh asked Utnapishtim for the secret to immortality. Utnapishtim told Gilgamesh how the gods, especially a god named Enlil, grew disgusted by mankind and decided to drown everyone in a flood. But one god, Ea, the god of wisdom, wanted to spare human beings. He instructed Utnapishtim to prepare for the flood by building a giant ship and loading his family and various animals inside. The heavens opened, and it poured rain for six days and nights. All people were drowned and turned into mud. On the seventh day, the ship rested on land, and Utnapishtim offered thanks to the gods. Enlil was furious that a human family survived, but Ea calmed him with kind words, and Enlil decided to grant Utnapishtim and his wife immortality as a peace offering.

After finishing his story, Utnapishtim challenged Gilgamesh to a test of endurance—if Gilgamesh could stay awake for seven days and six nights, Utnapishtim would grant him immortality. Gilgamesh, however, was so weary from his journeys that he soon fell asleep. When he awoke, Utnapishtim took pity on him. He told Gilgamesh of a prickly plant at the bottom of the sea that bestowed immortality on whomever ate it.

Overjoyed, Gilgamesh tied stones around his body and dove into the sea. He sank to the bottom, retrieved the plant, and set off for his homeland, convinced that neither he nor any of his people would ever die. Tragically, as Gilgamesh bathed in a pool during the journey home, a snake discovered the plant and ate it. Gilgamesh wept bitterly. He and his people would never escape the pain and darkness of death.

The Mesopotamians used this story to explain how snakes appear to have eternal life—because in reality, snakes shed their skins and look "young" again.

EGYPT

Who were the ancient Egyptians?

The ancient Egyptians were a people who settled on the banks of the Nile River in northern Africa. Almost 4,500 years ago, they created a magnificent empire that lasted nearly three thousand years.

What is the Egyptian myth of creation?

The universe began as a giant body of motionless water shrouded in darkness. The Egyptians called this lifeless body of water Nu, or Nun. From the depths of the water, a mound appeared, which was called the primeval mound. On it, the first Egyptian gods appeared.

This ancient Egyptian painting shows the Egyptian creation myth. Shu, the air god, stands supporting the body of Nut, the sky goddess, above Geb, the earth god.

Which Egyptian gods first appeared?

On top of the primeval mound, the first god came into being. He was the sun god, and most Egyptians called him Ra, or Ra-Atum. Ra created two gods called Shu and Tefnut by sneezing and spitting. Shu, god of the air, came from the sneeze. Tefnut, goddess of moisture, was created from Ra's saliva.

Who were Geb and Nut?

Shu and Tefnut gave birth to two gods—Geb and Nut. Geb was a male god who represented the land

Primeval Mound

The primeval mound is an important part of Egyptian culture. Archaeologists believe that Egyptians conceived the idea of the mound by watching the yearly flooding of the Nile River. When the river receded, small islands were uncovered.

Egyptians may have used this image in their creation myth to describe the waters of Nu and the appearance of the first land. The massive Egyptian pyramids also recall the primeval mound.

of Egypt. Lying on his back, the folds of Geb's body formed the mountains and valleys of the earth. Nut was a female sky goddess who stretched overhead in a large arc, forming the blue sky of day or shining with stars at night.

Originally, the two gods lay close to each other, making it impossible for any living thing to exist. Ra then ordered Shu, the god of the air, to separate them. Shu raised Nut so high that she began to tremble. During storms, the Egyptians believed that Nut slipped downward toward the earth, causing thunder.

Every day, Ra traveled in a sailing vessel, called the sun barque, along the underside of Nut's body. He began

Some Egyptian myths told how the sun god rose as a young boy out of a lotus flower that had grown on the primeval mound.

The Scarab Beetle

Egyptians were fascinated by the scarab beetle, which rolled together a small ball of dung. The next morning, as if by magic, baby beetles were born out of the ball (actually, the beetle had laid eggs). The scarab beetle became a sacred symbol of creation to the Egyptians, and in some myths, the sun was reborn as Khepry, the scarab beetle.

the journey as a young boy, grew into a man at noon, and was an old man in the evening. At dusk, Nut swallowed the sun barque with Ra inside. During the night hours, Nut's skin sparkled with stars as the sun god journeyed through her. At dawn, all creation was filled with joy as Nut gave birth to Ra, thus renewing the cycle of day and night. The blood she shed while giving birth colored the sunrise red.

How were other Egyptian gods born?

Geb and Nut were separated, but Nut was pregnant with Geb's children. Ra, angry that Geb and Nut had married in the first place, now noticed Nut's pregnancy and proclaimed that Nut could not give birth during any month of the year. To help Nut, Thoth, the god of learning, convinced the moon to add five extra days to the 360-day Egyptian year. During those five days, Nut gave birth to five children—Osiris, Horus the Elder, Isis, Seth, and Nephthys.

How were Egyptian men and women created?

According to one Egyptian myth, men and women were made by a ram-headed god named Khnum. Khnum took clay and molded a human body on a potter's wheel. Carefully, he created bones, blood vessels, a brain, a heart, and a stomach. When Khnum was finished, he presented a man and a woman to the sun god, who blessed them with life.

How was humankind almost destroyed?

Ruled by Ra, all Egyptian people prospered. But when Ra grew old and feeble, evil men plotted his downfall. Ra learned of their plans, and he called the other gods together for advice. The gods told him that humankind deserved to be destroyed. Heeding their words, Ra ordered the goddess Sakhmat to carry out his vengeance. Sakhmat was a fierce goddess with the head of a lioness and the body of a woman. Using her claws and razor-sharp teeth, she began slaughtering people by the tens of thousands. After one day, most of humankind was wiped out. But that night, as Sakhmat slept, Ra's anger cooled and he decided to spare the survivors.

Ra knew, however, that when Sakhmat awoke, she would be in such a frenzy that she would not obey his order to stop. To prevent more massacres, Ra ordered his servants to make seven thousand jars of beer and dye the beer red. Ra then dumped the beer into a giant pool. When Sakhmat woke, she believed the red beer was blood. Eagerly, she drank it until she became so full that she forgot about killing any more people. Humankind was saved.

But Ra was weary of the world and decided to end his rule. He continued to sail across the sky as the sun, and he created the moon to comfort people during the darkness of night. Ra chose the god Osiris to rule the world in his place.

Who was Osiris?

A handsome god with jet-black hair, Osiris was Egypt's first leader, a role he shared with his sister and wife, Isis. Osiris was a kind and wise king. He taught people how to raise crops and many other secrets of civilization. All of Egypt enjoyed his rule. But Osiris was locked in a struggle with his evil brother, Seth, the god of chaos. Seth grew jealous of his brother's success as a king and plotted to murder him.

How was Osiris murdered?

Osiris left Egypt to teach men and women throughout the world the secrets of farming and civilization. While he was gone, his faithful wife Isis ruled in his place. When Osiris at last returned, Seth invited him to a grand banquet. During the celebration, Seth displayed a magnificent chest covered with decorations. Seth told his guests that the chest belonged to whoever could fit into it exactly.

Each guest tried to fit into the chest. Some were too tall, others were too short. Finally, it was Osiris's turn. He fit perfectly. As he lay there, Seth suddenly slammed the lid shut and sealed the chest with molten lead. He heaved the chest into the Nile River, where it swiftly floated

This ancient Egyptian stone carving depicts the divine royal family. Horus, on the left, has a male body and the head of a falcon. Osiris stands in the middle with his faithful wife, Isis, to the right.

downstream and out of sight. Osiris suffocated inside the chest, and Seth became the king of Egypt.

How did Isis give birth to Osiris's son?

Devastated by her husband's death, Isis frantically began searching for his body. She learned from farmers and sailors that the chest had floated out to the Mediterranean Sea and had come ashore in present-day Lebanon. There, a tree had grown around it, enfolding the chest within its roots and bark. A king had noticed the size and beauty of the tree, and he had it cut down to be used as a pillar in his palace.

Isis went to the palace and recovered the coffin. Returning to Egypt, she used magic to revive Osiris long enough to conceive a child. Now pregnant, Isis fled to the marshes of the Nile delta to hide from Seth. There she gave birth to a son—Horus.

Who was Horus?

Horus, son of Isis and Osiris, was from his birth destined to avenge his father's murder. Nurtured and protected by Isis, Horus grew into a strong warrior with a falcon's head and a man's body. Seth learned of Horus's existence, and he searched the Nile delta to kill him. Seth did not find Horus, but he did stumble upon the casket containing Osiris's body. Enraged at the fact that Isis had tricked him, Seth cut Osiris's body into fourteen pieces and scattered them throughout Egypt.

Isis patiently searched for and recovered almost all of Osiris's body. (According to Egyptian legend, a temple was built on each spot where a piece of Osiris was discovered.) Isis used her magic and craft to put the body back together—Egypt's first mummy.

Did Horus ever challenge Seth?

When Horus was old enough, he challenged Seth for the throne of Egypt. The two gods clashed in terrible warfare. Horus won many victories, but Seth was cunning and always escaped. Finally, Seth and Horus agreed to stop fighting and to settle the issue before an assembly of the gods.

The trial lasted eighty years as both Horus and Seth tried to convince the assembly that they had the right to Osiris's throne. Isis grew impatient and addressed the gods, winning their sympathy to Horus's cause. Infuriated, Seth vowed not to participate in any court where Isis was present. Ra agreed with Seth's demand. He moved the assembly to an island and ordered the ferryman not to carry any woman on his boat.

How did Isis help Horus become king?

Isis was determined to get on the island. She used magic to turn herself into an old woman and asked the ferryman to take her to the island. Believing that the old woman could not possibly be Isis, the ferryman agreed.

Once she arrived, Isis transformed herself into a beautiful young woman. She asked Seth for help, claiming that her husband was dead and that her son's cattle had been stolen. Seth agreed to help, saying that it was wicked for a son to be deprived of his inheritance. Hearing these words, Isis changed into a bird and flew into a tree. She told Seth that by his own statements he had condemned himself.

The court awarded Horus the throne of Egypt, and Osiris became god of the underworld. Ra took Seth into the sky with him, where Seth became the god of thunder and storms.

How did the pharaohs pay homage to Horus?

The Egyptians believed that the pharaoh was the descendant of Ra and that he became Horus when he ruled over Egypt. In this way, the pharaoh was considered a god while still on earth.

What did the Egyptians believe happened to common people in the afterlife?

When an Egyptian who was not a member of the royal family died, his soul had to travel through a series of rigorous tests to arrive in paradise, called the Field of Reeds. The climax of the journey occurred when the soul was brought before Osiris, the supreme judge of the afterlife. While Osiris watched from his throne, the soul's heart was weighed on a giant scale against a symbol of truth and justice. If the heart was evil, the soul was condemned to a horrible fate. If the heart was pure, then the soul could joyfully enter paradise.

SUB-SAHARAN AFRICA

What is African mythology?

Africa is home to hundreds of different peoples, who have developed many complex mythologies and stories. Most of these tales were passed down from one generation to the next by word of mouth. The particular culture or area that the myth comes from is noted in parentheses after the question.

How was the world created? (Yoruba)

At the beginning of time, the universe was divided into two regions—the sky and an endless stretch of water and marsh. Many gods lived in the sky world, but only one cared about the vast stretch of water beneath. His name was Obatala. Obatala asked Olorun, ruler of the sky, if he could cover the water with land so people could live there. Olorun supported the idea, but he doubted anyone could complete such a momentous task. With Olorun's permission, Obatala took a gold chain and hung it from the sky down to the water world. But the chain wasn't long enough to reach the water. Obatala climbed down to the end of the chain, hearing the crash of waves through the dark, damp mist below him. He took a snail shell filled with sand from his pack and poured it into the mist. Next, he dropped a hen, which landed on the sand and began to kick it in all directions. The sand turned into dry land. In some places, the sand collected into piles and became mountains. In other places, the sand sank and became valleys.

How were people created? (Yoruba)

Now that there was land, Obatala planted a palm nut that grew into the first tree. This tree scattered its nuts, and soon the ground sprouted many kinds of plants. From high above in the sky, Olorun watched Obatala with great interest. He sent down a chameleon to ask Obatala if he needed anything. Obatala replied that everything was going well, except that it was too dark. Olorun fashioned the sun and set it in the dome of the sky.

Despite feeling satisfaction with his world, Obatala grew lonely. He decided to make people. Scraping mud and clay from the ground, Obatala molded the first figures. The work was hard and difficult, and Obatala grew thirsty. To refresh himself, he drank wine—too much wine. When he went back to his work, Obatala was drunk. Clumsily, he molded some figures with crooked backs and arms and legs that were too short. Some did not have enough fingers and toes. Others were bent over instead of standing straight. When Obatala had made enough figures, Olorun gave them life. When the new people began moving, Obatala observed with horror that many of them were crippled. He swore never to drink wine again, and he vowed to protect all people who suffer from deformities.

How did Sogbo become god of the thunderstorm? (Fon)

After creating the world and the universe, the goddess Mawu let her two sons, Sagbata and Sogbo, rule over it. The brothers, however, bitterly argued. Finally, in a fit of rage, Sagbata left the sky world to live on earth. As Sagbata packed his things together in a bag, he realized that if he packed water and fire, fire would burn his belongings and water would soak them. Reluctantly, Sagbata left fire and water in the sky. Sogbo was delighted with Sagbata's departure. As ruler of the sky world, he controlled thunder, fire, rain, and, most important, the lightning bolt.

After Sagbata left, Sogbo decided to assert his power over his brother. He refused to send the clouds into the sky, and not a drop of rain fell for a year. Down on earth, the people watched in a panic as their crops withered and died. They approached Sagbata and demanded to know what was happening. But Sagbata didn't know. He could only hope that it would rain soon.

But it did not. The drought went on for three more years. In desperation, Sagbata summoned Sogbo's messenger, the bird Watutu, and asked him why his brother did not send rain. Watutu replied that Sogbo would be satisfied with part of Sagbata's wealth on earth. Realizing that he had no choice, Sagbata agreed. Immediately, thunder cracked and rain poured down onto the dry and dusty earth.

The Fon people learned an important lesson from this story. Humankind is at the mercy of the gods and must pay them respect.

Why do people die? (Nuer)

Where the Nuer people live, a rope once dropped out of heaven and reached the earth. Any old person could climb up the rope into heaven and return to earth as a young person. In those times, people lived forever. But one day, a hyena climbed the rope. The High God in

The Yoruba god of thunder and lightening, Shango, is carved on this wooden staff used by a priest in religious ceremonies to ward off the area's frequent rainstorms. The god Shango is always depicted with a double axe-shaped headdress.

heaven ordered the hyena to remain in heaven, because he would certainly cause trouble on earth. After dark, however, the hyena slipped out of heaven and climbed back down the rope. When he neared the ground, the hyena cut the rope. The rope above the cut was drawn back into heaven, severing the connection between heaven and earth. Thus, people can no longer visit heaven to replenish their youth. Instead, they die.

How did the Ostrich get its long neck? (Kikuyu)

Originally, the ostrich had a short neck, just like a duck or a partridge. One day, a male ostrich told his wife that he would rest on the eggs for one evening. The wife, weary from sitting for several weeks, was thrilled. While her husband made himself comfortable, she pranced about their nest in joy. Later that night, the ostrich heard his wife laughing with another male ostrich. Furious, he prepared to jump up and accuse her of wrongdoing, when he suddenly remembered the valuable eggs beneath him. Instead, he strained his neck to glimpse her above the tall grass, but he saw nothing. He heard her giggles and tried again. This time, he just glimpsed her as she raced past. For the rest of the night, the ostrich desperately looked for his wife in vain. In the morning, the ostrich was surprised to find that his neck had stretched and stretched until it rose far above the grass. The ostrich's neck has been long ever since.

How did the Hare clear his fields? (West Africa)

One day, Hare decided to get married. But he encountered a problem—Hare hated to work, and he needed to clear a field and plant crops to support a wife. His field was covered with thick, tangled bushes, and the task appeared hopeless. Then, Hare had an idea. He took a rope and challenged an enormous hippopotamus to a game of tug-of-war. Hippo readily agreed, and Hare tied the rope around Hippo's body. "When you feel me pull," said Hare, "pull back." Hare then disappeared into the jungle and found Elephant. This time, he challenged Elephant to a tug-of-war. Chuckling to himself, Elephant said yes. Hare tied the rope around Elephant's neck and walked back into the forest. When he reached the middle of the rope, Hare pulled in both directions. Both creatures lurched forward and strained at the rope. Amazed that a tiny hare had such strength, Elephant and Hippo tugged and pulled, violently heaving this way and that. The struggle lasted all day. By sundown, the rope had ripped down the bushes and softened the ground. Hare now owned a cleared field and could easily plant crops.

How did Monkey trick Shark? (West Africa)

Monkey lived in a tall tree by the ocean. Bushels of sweet fruit called mangoes grew in the tree. Whenever he was hungry, Monkey hopped through the branches and ate the delicious fruit. Sometimes, he threw the mangoes into the ocean and was delighted by the giant splash. Swimming beneath the waves, Shark enjoyed eating the fruit. One day, he rose to the ocean surface and asked Monkey to come with him to his home. Monkey looked nervously at Shark's razor-sharp teeth and told him that he hated to get wet. Shark told Monkey to grab his fin and ride on his back. That way, he promised, not a drop would touch him. Reluctantly, Monkey agreed, and soon the two were racing across the ocean.

When land had disappeared from sight, Shark told him that his chief was sick. The sharks had given the chief everything to eat, but nothing made him better. Finally, they had agreed that a monkey's heart would be the cure. When he heard this, Monkey clutched his chest and groaned. "I didn't bring my heart!" he cried. Shark was stunned and asked where it was. Monkey told him that it was back in the tree, where he had hung it up for safe-keeping. Monkey convinced Shark to return to shore, where Monkey would get his heart and climb back onto Shark's back to help the king.

But when Monkey jumped into the tree, he didn't reappear for several hours. Tired of waiting, Shark asked Monkey what took him so long. Safe among the tree branches, Monkey mocked Shark, telling him that his heart had been in his chest all along. Shark returned without a cure for his chief. Since then, monkeys never swim in the ocean.

The Trickster

African myths often describe a small and weak character defeating a stronger opponent through cunning and trickery. This mythological figure is called "the trickster." Tricksters are popular characters in many world mythologies, including Norse (Loki) and North American Indian (Coyote). African American folklore tells the antics of "Brer Rabbit," a small rabbit who outsmarts larger and more powerful animals. West Africans brought stories of the cunning rabbit to North America when they arrived in the United States as slaves.

How did Mantis get fire? (San)

One day, Mantis smelled a wonderful aroma floating through the countryside. Curious, Mantis peeked through a bush and saw Ostrich roasting food over a fire. When Ostrich finished eating, he took the fire and tucked it under his wing. Mantis had never seen fire, and he now wanted it for himself. When Ostrich jogged by, Mantis called out to him and told him of a wonderful tree filled with fruit. Excited, Ostrich followed Mantis to a tree covered with yellow plums. "The best fruit," said Mantis, "is at the top." Ostrich eagerly reached up with his long neck and extended his wings to keep his balance. As soon as Ostrich opened his wings, Mantis snatched the fire and fled. Since then, Ostrich has kept its wings at its side and has never attempted to fly.

Who were the ancient Greeks? ♦ How did the ancient
Greeks believe their world and universe began? ♦ Who
were the Titans? ♦ What happened to the Titans? ♦
When did the gods create men? ♦ How did Prometheus
help the creation of men and the first woman? ♦
What was Pandora's Box? ♦ What happened to
Prometheus? ♦ How did the Greeks explain the
changing of the seasons? ♦ Who was Herakles? ♦ Who
was Perseus? ♦ What were the Gorgons? ♦ How did
Perseus slay Medusa? ♦ Who was Jason? ♦ What was
the Golden Fleece? ♦ How did Jason retrieve the Golden
Fleece? ♦ Who was Theseus? ♦ What was the Minotaur?

MEDITERRANEAN CULTURES

GREECE

Who were the ancient Greeks?

The ancient Greeks lived throughout the Greek
peninsula and islands and along the nearby coasts of the
Mediterranean Sea. They thrived from 800 B.C. until 133
B.C., when Roman armies conquered Greece. During those
centuries, the Greeks created a glorious civilization of art,
literature, and architecture that still inspires and influences
Western civilization today. The myths they told are among
the most colorful, beautiful, and challenging stories ever
created.

How did the ancient Greeks believe their world and universe began?

The ancient Greeks believed that the universe began
as a confusing, dark, and formless chaos. Nothing existed.
Out of this chaos emerged the being from which all life
began—Mother Earth, called Gaea. Gaea gave birth to the
stunning blue vault of heaven sprinkled with stars. The
heaven was called Uranus.

Uranus and Gaea had many children. Some of them
towered above the landscape and saw the world through a
single giant eye set in the middle of their foreheads. They

were called Cyclopes. Other children had more than one hundred hands and fifty heads. Uranus was especially disgusted with these creatures, and he imprisoned them deep within the earth. Horrifed by Uranus's actions, Gaea asked the Cyclopes and another group of her children, called the Titans, to help her.

Who were the Titans?

The Titans were twelve children born to Gaea and Uranus. Six were male and six were female (the women were called Titanesses). They were powerful creatures that stood as tall as mountains. When Gaea asked the Titans for help against Uranus, only one was bold enough—Cronus. Wielding a sickle-shaped sword, Cronus attacked his father and drove the sword into his body. Seriously wounded, Uranus fled from his son and never challenged him again.

Cronus now ruled the universe with his sister, Rhea. Together, they also had several children. But Cronus feared that one of his children would dethrone him in the future. To prevent this, he swallowed each child as it was born. Cronus's immortal children continued to live trapped within his body. Bitter and angry at the loss of her children, Rhea resolved to keep one from Cronus. When she gave birth to her sixth child—a boy—she hid him in Crete, an island in the Mediterranean Sea. She wrapped a stone in baby clothes and gave it to Cronus, who thought the stone was the newborn child and quickly swallowed it.

Unknown to Cronus, his son—called Zeus—grew strong on Crete and plotted to overthrow his father. When he was old enough, Zeus took a Titaness called Metis for his wife. To aid her new husband, Metis tricked Cronus into eating an herb by telling him that the herb would make him invincible. It didn't. Instead, it made him violently sick. Cronus vomited up his five children and the giant stone. Zeus and his brothers and sisters now attacked Cronus and drove him from power.

The other Titans challenged Zeus's rule, and war broke out between the two groups. To help his cause, Zeus liberated the monsters that Uranus had imprisoned

within the earth. Grateful for their freedom, they fashioned a mighty thunderbolt for Zeus to use in battle.
Armed with such a weapon, Zeus led his brothers and
sisters to victory over the Titans.

What happened to the Titans?

Zeus punished some of the Titans severely. One
Titan, called Atlas, was forced to bear the crushing weight
of the earth and heavens upon his shoulders forever.

The Spanish painter Francisco
de Goya (1746–1828) painted
this gruesome picture of
Saturn (or Cronus) devouring
his children.

The Olympians

The Olympians are the twelve gods that ruled the universe after the Titans were defeated in battle. They lived in luxury in a splendid palace atop Mount Olympus, a mountain that towered over the world and where no snow or rain ever fell. Within the halls of the palace, the gods feasted, drank, listened to music, conversed, and quarreled.

Zeus was the unchallenged leader of the Olympians. With his mighty thunderbolt, he subdued his enemies and demanded obedience from all people and gods. But Zeus shared some power with the other eleven Olympians. Each god and goddess had a distinct personality and was concerned with a different activity in the lives of men and women.

Zeus's brother Poseidon ruled the sea. Except for Zeus, he was the most powerful god. Carrying a mighty trident, Poseidon could shatter ships and batter cities with tidal waves and earthquakes. He could also gentle a stormy sea with one sweep of his hand. The Greeks were expert sailors who relied upon the sea both for food and trade. They deeply revered Poseidon.

Hades was also Zeus's brother. A gloomy and solitary god, he ruled the underworld where the souls of the dead gathered for eternity.

Hera was Zeus's sister and wife. She was especially concerned with the institution of marriage, married women, and childbirth. The name *Hera* means lady in Greek. Many of her stories show her pursuing Zeus

Other Titans were flung into a dark region beneath the earth called Tartarus.

Zeus had children with Mnemosyne, the Titaness of memory. The children were nine daughters called Muses. The Muses inspired great thought, especially in music, art, literature, and dance.

Zeus also had three daughters with the Titaness Eurynome. The children became the three Charites (they were also called Graces) who represented beauty, gentleness, and friendship.

Zeus left some Titans alone. The Titan Oceanus continued to circle the earth as a giant river. The Titan Prometheus had joined Zeus in the war against the Titans. His shrewd advice helped Zeus to victory. Later, Prometheus would become very important to humankind.

The word music *comes from the Greek word* muse.

and his many lovers with fierce vengeance.

Apollo was the son of Zeus and god of light and truth. He also inspired music and art, guided the arrows of archers, and controlled the art of healing. Greeks visited his oracle at Delphi to learn of future events and to understand the will of the gods.

Artemis was Apollo's twin sister. Like her brother, Artemis was an expert hunter who shot arrows with perfect accuracy.

Athena was the daughter of Zeus and the goddess of wisdom. Her mother was the Titaness Metis. Zeus had learned that a son born from Metis would overthrow him, so he swallowed Metis after he discovered that she was pregnant with his child. Metis gave birth to Athena inside Zeus, and Athena sprang fully formed out of Zeus's skull.

Aphrodite, the goddess of love and beauty, was born from a foaming wave in the sea. Her son, Eros, shot arrows into the hearts of lovers to fan their passion.

Ares, the son of Zeus and Hera, was the god of war. Ares was a fickle and ruthless god who inspired arguments and bloodshed.

Hephaistos was Ares's brother. Ugly and lame, Hephaistos was god of crafts and created many beautiful and ingenious devices for the gods.

Hermes, also Zeus's son, was the messenger of the gods. Using his winged sandals, Hermes carried messages, helped people on their journeys, and guided the dead to the underworld.

When did the gods create men?

The Titan Prometheus fashioned the first men out of clay and water. Prometheus allowed his brother Epimetheus to give qualities to animals and man. Dull and stupid, Epimetheus gave speed, strength, courage, and many other characteristics to the animals and left nothing to man. Prometheus was very upset, and he gave mankind one redeeming quality—the ability to walk upright like the gods.

How did Prometheus help men?

Prometheus took delight in his creation, and he sought to shelter man against the wrath of Zeus. Prometheus saw that men had to sacrifice food to the gods, sometimes so much that they had none left over for themselves. Prometheus decided to help man by making Zeus choose between two animal sacrifices. He took the best meat from the sacrifice and wrapped it in an ugly piece of skin and fur. Prometheus then wrapped the bones and fur in a piece of juicy fat. Zeus looked over the two piles and selected the one that looked the best—the one wrapped in fat. He was enraged to discover the bones and fur underneath. Because of Zeus's decision, the Greeks sacrificed the worst part of the animal—the skin and bones—to the gods, while keeping the meatiest portions for themselves.

Angry at being deceived, Zeus deprived mankind of fire. Prometheus saw men shivering in the darkness and had pity. He secretly took a coal from Hephaistos's forge and gave it to man.

Why did Zeus create the first woman?

Zeus was furious when he saw men with fire and vowed revenge. This time, Zeus ordered Hephaistos to create a person who would use deceit and trickery to disrupt the society of men—a woman.

Hephaistos mixed clay and water and carefully molded a female figure. When he was finished, the goddesses of Mount Olympus gathered to shower her with gifts. Athena adorned her in lovely robes. Other goddesses placed sparkling necklaces of gold around her neck and a crown of flowers on her head. Aphrodite gave her beauty and grace. But the god Hermes gave her the ability to lie. Her name was Pandora, which means the gift of all.

What was Pandora's Box?

Zeus gave Pandora a box and warned her never to open it. But Pandora grew curious. Everyday she looked at the box and longed to know what was inside. Finally, she could no longer resist, and she opened the box. The lid flew open and a host of misery, sickness, and mischief spread out into the world. Horrified, Pandora slammed the chest shut, but everything had escaped except for one thing—hope. Even today, in the midst of misfortune and disaster, men and women still have hope.

What happened to Prometheus?

Zeus wanted some information from Prometheus. Prometheus could see into the future, and he knew which of Zeus's sons would rise up and defeat him. But Prometheus refused to tell Zeus. In a fury, Zeus chained Prometheus to a mountain and sent a giant eagle to tear Prometheus's liver from his body. Because he was immortal, Prometheus's liver grew back every night. Everyday, the eagle returned for his grisly meal. Despite his agony, Prometheus never gave Zeus the information he demanded.

How did the Greeks explain the changing of the seasons?

Demeter, goddess of all plants that grew and bloomed on the earth, cherished her only daughter—Persephone. One day, while walking through some fields, Persephone was seized by Hades, god of the underworld, and taken down into the earth on his chariot. Demeter was crushed with grief by the disappearance of her daughter. As she searched for Persephone, nothing grew on the earth, and

On the interior of this Greek bowl, two titans are shown being punished for defying Zeus. On the left, Atlas strains to hold up the world while he tries to soothe his aching back. On the right, Prometheus is bound to a tree as an eagle tears out his liver. This bowl was decorated in the popular black figure style, circa 4th century B.C., in which the black color of the glazed clay forms the figures while the background and details are painted.

humankind suffered through a devastating famine. The other gods pleaded with Demeter, but she refused to allow any flowers to bloom or any trees to bear fruit until she held her daughter again.

Zeus ordered Hades to free Persephone. As long as Persephone had eaten nothing in the underworld, she would be released. But Hades tricked Persephone into eating six pomegranate seeds. Consequently, Zeus decided that Persephone had to spend six months of every year with Hades in his dark realm. During the six months when Persephone was gone each year, Demeter pined for her daughter, and all of earth lay barren in the grip of winter. When Persephone returned,

Herakles, wearing a lion skin and wielding his club, battles the deadly Hydra in this late 19th century illustration. The myths of the Greeks have inspired artists of all eras and cultures for more than two millennia.

Demeter expressed her joy as the plant life burst into the bloom of spring.

Who was Herakles?

The son of Zeus and a mortal woman, Herakles (also known as Hercules) was the strongest man in ancient Greece. The goddess Hera, always jealous of Zeus's love affairs, learned about the child and sent two giant snakes to kill him as he lay in his crib at night. When the snakes appeared, Herakles grasped them in his powerful hands and strangled them.

Herakles' temper was as great as his strength, and he could fly into a rage with devastating results. Once, Herakles suffered a blinding madness that caused him to murder his wife and three children. When he had realized what he had done, the grief-stricken Herakles visited Apollo's oracle in Delphi to learn how to pay for his crime. The oracle ordered Herakles to travel to his cousin, King Eurystheus. There, Herakles was to serve the king in any way the king saw fit. When King Eurystheus was satisfied with Herakles' penance, he would be free of his crime. Herakles' penance consisted of what are now known as the Twelve Labors of Herakles.

King Eurystheus was a shrewd but cowardly ruler, and he took great delight in the fact that the strongest man in the world was now his slave. Eagerly, he devised new difficult labors for Herakles as fast as the hero completed them.

Many of the labors pitted Herakles against monsters and deadly animals. In one labor, Herakles traveled to the swamps of Lerna to kill the immortal Hydra monster—a huge snake with nine heads. When Herakles found the Hydra, he swiftly struck at the swirling, hissing heads with his arrow and clubs. But each time he destroyed one head, two more heads sprung up in its place. Desperate, Herakles asked his young nephew, Iolaus, to set a burning branch on each shattered head. This tactic worked, and Herakles pinned the decapitated body of the Hydra under a giant rock.

For other labors, Herakles had to complete nearly impossible tasks. King Eurystheus ordered Herakles to

Herakles *is a Greek word, which means Glory of Hera.*

clean out the Augean stables in one day. Home to thousands of cattle and horses, the Augean stables had not been cleaned in years. Herakles performed the labor by diverting two mighty rivers into the stables. The rush of water washed away the filthy piles of dung, leaving the stables clean.

King Eurystheus also challenged Herakles to retrieve magical items from distant realms. Herakles had to bring him the Golden Apples of Hesperides from a sacred garden guarded by goddesses. To find out where the garden was, Herakles asked Atlas, father of the Hesperides, to help him. Atlas still strained under the weight of the earth and heavens. He told Herakles to take his place briefly, and he would fetch the apples for him. Herakles agreed. But when Atlas came back with the apples, he told Herakles that he was weary with holding the heavens and earth and that it was now Herakles' job. Herakles asked Atlas to take back the weight briefly. He explained that his shoulders were sore and that he needed to adjust his robe for comfort. Atlas, simple and dull, took up the crushing weight once more, and Herakles hurried off with the apples.

For his twelfth and final labor, Herakles was told to capture the three-headed dog, Cerberus, who guarded the gate to the underworld. Hades, god of the underworld, told Herakles to take the dog, but only if he did not use any weapons. Herakles wrestled with the beast, finally dragging it before King Eurystheus. The king sensibly told Herakles to put Cerebus back where he had found it.

Who was Perseus?

Perseus was the son of Zeus and a mortal woman. As a young man, he attended a king's banquet where the king requested a gift from each of his guests. Each of the other guests offered a horse. But Perseus, who was broke, could only offer his services. The king demanded that Perseus bring him the head of a Gorgon.

What were the Gorgons?

The Gorgons were hideous snake-haired female monsters. Their necks were covered with the scales of a dragon, they bristled with sharp tusks, and they had hands of bronze and wings of gold. A glance from any of the three

The Hero

Heroes thrill us with their daring, strength, and courage. They also teach and inspire us to accomplish what others consider impossible. Cultures around the world tell of the exploits of heroes. The Greeks shared stories of Herakles, Theseus, and Jason. The Babylonians idolized Gilgamesh. In India, the hero Rama battled and defeated forces of evil.

Gorgons turned the viewer to stone. Only three Gorgons lived in the world, and they stayed hidden in a cave so no one would behold their terrible features. They were named Medusa, Stheno, and Euryale. Two were immortal, but Medusa had originally been a beautiful mortal woman. She performed an act of disrespect to the goddess Athena when the god Poseidon seduced her in Athena's temple. The angry goddess cursed her beauty and transformed her fair features into twisted images of horror.

How did Perseus slay Medusa?

Luckily for Perseus, many gods hated the Gorgons and helped Perseus in his quest. The goddess Athena told Perseus to visit the Graeae to find out where the Gorgons lived. The Graeae were three old women who shared one eye and one tooth among them. Perseus made the unwilling witches help him on his quest by snatching the eye and refusing to return it until they had divulged the secret location of the Gorgon's lair. Perseus also received invaluable help from some nymphs, who gave him a cap of darkness that made him invisible, winged sandals that allowed him to fly, and a leather bag. The god Hermes provided him with a razor-sharp curved sword.

Perseus flew to a cave far in the west where the Gorgons lived. Using his shield as a mirror to keep from being turned to stone, he approached the sleeping Medusa and lopped off her head with one powerful stroke. Medusa's sisters awoke and searched for the murderous intruder, but Perseus donned his cap of invisibility and escaped.

As he journeyed home, Perseus saw a beautiful young woman, named Andromeda, chained to a rock by the sea. Andromeda was being sacrificed to a sea monster because her mother had boastfully praised Andromeda's beauty above the Nereids, a group of sea nymphs who were dear to Poseidon. Perseus was enchanted by Andromeda's beauty, and he promised to kill the sea monster if Andromeda would become his wife.

When the monster appeared, Perseus wore his cap of invisibility and cut open the monster's throat. The hideous beast fell back into the sea and disappeared beneath the waves. Overjoyed, Perseus claimed Andromeda as his wife. But Andromeda's other suitors grew jealous of Perseus, and they plotted to seize Andromeda and take her away. Seeing the suitors charge, Perseus held Medusa's severed head aloft and turned them to stone. When Perseus and Andromeda died years later, the goddess Athena placed them in the night sky as constellations, where they can still be seen today.

Who was Jason?

Jason was a hero whose travels took him to the ends of the earth. When Jason was a young man, he agreed to carry an old woman across a river. The old woman was the goddess Hera in disguise, and Jason enjoyed Hera's gratitude and protection for the rest of his life.

Jason's father was once a great king. But his father's brother stole the throne, and when Jason grew to be a young man, he traveled to regain his father's kingdom. When he reached the land, Jason boldly announced his intentions to King Pelias. Pelias was terrified of Jason and planned to get rid of him by sending him on an impossible mission. The king agreed to surrender the throne if Jason could complete one task—recovering the Golden Fleece. Jason accepted the challenge and gathered his comrades together.

What was the Golden Fleece?

The Golden Fleece was a coat of fur from a sacred bull that had been sent by Zeus to rescue a child about to be sacrificed by his father. The bull swooped down to the altar, placed the boy on his back, and escaped. The bull carried the boy to Colchis, a kingdom ruled by King Aeetes on the eastern coast of the Black Sea. The king was stunned by the bull's beautiful thick golden coat and recognized it as a gift from the gods. He sacrificed the bull to Zeus and hung its golden coat in a sacred grove, where it was guarded by a dragon that never slept.

How did Jason retrieve the Golden Fleece?

Jason and his comrades, called the Argonauts, built a mighty ship—the *Argo*—to carry them safely through the long journey. They sailed through many adventures before arriving in Colchis and appearing before King Aeetes. King Aeetes despised Greeks, and he told Jason that he would slaughter all of them. Calmly, Jason told the king that he would complete any task in exchange for the Golden Fleece. The king challenged Jason to yoke two fire-breathing bulls and sow a field with dragon's teeth.

To help Jason, the goddess Hera made King Aeetes' lovely daughter, Medea, fall in love with Jason. Medea was a skilled sorceress, and she gave Jason magical potions and the secrets he needed to perform his task. With this knowledge, he was able to subdue the fire-breathing bulls and plant dragon's teeth in the plowed furrows. Immediately after he had planted the teeth, armed warriors grew up from the ground. Following Medea's advice, Jason threw a stone in the midst of them. Each warrior accused the other of throwing the rock, and they stabbed and hacked each other until none were left alive.

But King Aeetes had no intention of honoring his pledge to Jason, and he plotted to massacre Jason and his crew while they slept. Suspecting her father's treachery, Medea urged Jason to take the fleece before dawn. Together, they stole into the sacred grove where the fleece hung in a tree. Medea cast a spell on the guardian dragon, sending it into a deep slumber. Jason quickly seized the fleece and hurried with Medea back to the *Argo*, where they roused the crew and escaped from Colchis.

Who was Theseus?

Before Theseus was born, his father, King Aegeus of Athens, traveled to the Delphic oracle. The oracle warned Aegeus not to open his wine flask before he returned home. Not understanding the message, Aegeus got drunk on his way back to Athens and slept with a woman named Aethra. When Aegeus realized she was pregnant, he took a sword and sandals and placed them under a rock. He told Aethra not to tell the child who his father was, but when he was strong enough to lift the rock and retrieve the sword and sandals, she should send him to Athens.

Theseus grew into a strong young man. When he was old enough, Aethra took him to the rock and told him about his father. Realizing that he was the heir to the Athenian throne, Theseus lifted the rock, took the sandals and sword, and set off for Athens. By then, King Aegeus had grown old and feeble and many Athenians plotted to seize his throne. He was overjoyed when he recognized Theseus wearing the sandals and holding the sword he had placed under the rock. After defeating Aegeus's enemies, Theseus told his father that he would kill a monster that had threatened Athens for decades—the Minotaur.

What was the Minotaur?

The Minotaur was a terrifying monster that was half man and half bull. It lived in a long and intricate maze, called the Labyrinth, that burrowed for miles underground on the island of Crete. King Minos of Crete demanded that Athens send seven young men and seven young women to be sacrificed to the Minotaur every year. The unfortunate sacrifices were locked in the Labyrinth, where they wandered lost until devoured by the Minotaur.

Theseus asked his father to allow him to be chosen as one of the youths to be sacrificed. He promised to slay the monster. Aegeus made Theseus swear that, upon his return, he would hoist a white sail to let his father know that he was safe.

How did Theseus defeat the Minotaur?

When Theseus arrived in Crete, Ariadne, the daughter of King Minos, fell in love with the hero. She gave Theseus a sword and a ball of thread, which he tied to a stone at the Labyrinth's entrance before he wandered inside in search of the monster. Theseus found the Minotaur and killed him.

With the Minotaur dead, Theseus gathered the other Athenians together and followed the thread out of the cave. They hurried to the ships and set sail for home. Heartlessly, Theseus abandoned the faithful Ariadne at a nearby island. In his haste, Theseus forgot to replace the ship's black sail with a white one. King Aegeus glimpsed the black sail from a cliff and plunged into the sea in grief. With the death of the old king, Theseus became king of Athens.

Who were Daedalus and Icarus?

A brilliant craftsman and designer, Daedalus designed the intricate Labyrinth that held the Minotaur. After Theseus killed the Minotaur, King Minos imprisoned Daedalus and his son, Icarus, because he suspected that Daedalus had revealed the secret of the Labyrinth to Ariadne. To escape, Daedalus fashioned two sets of wings out of wax and feathers. Just before soaring into the air, Daedalus sternly warned his son to avoid flying too close to the sun. But as the two men flew, Icarus felt overjoyed by flight. He climbed higher and higher, until the sun's heat melted the wax that held the feathers together. His wings fell apart and Icarus plunged to his death. Daedalus flew on with a heavy heart and arrived safely on the island of Sicily.

Who were Orpheus and Eurydice?

Except for the gods, no one played music as skillfully or beautifully as Orpheus. His singing made the trees bend closer and the stones gather around to listen. Orpheus fell in love with Eurydice, a nymph he wooed with his songs. But on the day of their wedding, Eurydice was bit by a poisonous snake and as Orpheus watched in horror and grief, his new wife died in his arms.

Orpheus was determined to bring his wife back from the dead, and he plunged into the cold and fierce

The sea into which the mythological King Aegeus fell is still known as the Aegean Sea.

underworld. There, he calmed all spirits and monsters with his music. Finally, he stood before Hades and his wife, Persephone, and pleaded for the return of his wife. Even Hades could not resist a request so beautifully sung. Persephone convinced Hades to give Orpheus his wife with one condition: Orpheus could not look back at Euridyce until both of them were safely out of the underworld. Eagerly, Orpheus agreed, and the two began the journey back to the world of the living.

Orpheus longed to take just one glance back at his beloved wife, to make sure that she was there. Finally, he reached the entrance to the underworld and stepped into the sunlight. He turned and looked back, but Eurydice was still in the shadows of the underworld, and all she could say was "farewell" before she disappeared again. Frantic, Orpheus tried to follow, but the gods would not allow a mortal to enter the underworld twice. Devastated, Orpheus was left alone with the knowledge that he had lost his love.

After ignoring his father's warning to fly low and away from the sun, Icarus plunges to his death while his father looks on helplessly. Italian artist Carlo Saraceni (1585–1620) painted this striking version of the well-known myth.

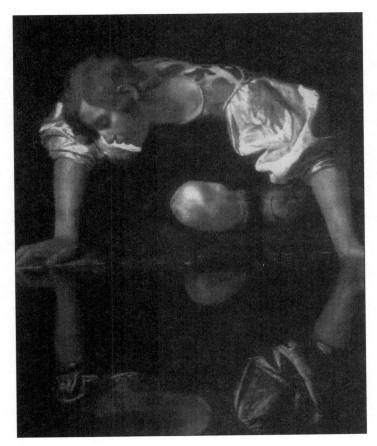

Narcissus glimpses his own reflection in a pool and falls desperately in love. He will remain there, wasting away until he is transformed into a flower. Caravaggio (1573–1610), an influential Italian painter, created this work, one of numerous depictions of the perennially popular myth.

Who were Narcissus and Echo?

Echo was a nymph who delighted in conversation. One day, Hera suspected that Zeus had fallen in love with a nymph. She approached a group of nymphs, determined to discover which one was guilty of attracting Zeus. As she drew near, Echo suddenly spoke to the goddess, amusing her with her chatter until the others escaped. When Hera realized Echo's trickery, she angrily struck the nymph's tongue dead except to repeat the words of others.

Sadly, Echo fell in love with a youth named Narcissus, who was the most beautiful young man in Greece. Wherever he traveled, he received exclamations of admiration and sighs of love. But Narcissus was filled with pride, and he coldly rejected all of them. Echo, lovesick and ignored, could

The word narcissistic *describes those who are absorbed in their own beauty or circumstances.*

only follow him silently except to repeat the words he spoke. Finally, Echo wasted away until only her voice remained.

One rejected nymph prayed that Narcissus would suffer for his cold pride by feeling the pain of unrequited love. The god Nemesis heard her prayer. After a long day of hunting, Narcissus leaned over a pool to drink. Suddenly, Narcissus glimpsed his own image on the surface staring back at him. Entranced, Narcissus leaned over to grasp the image, but his hands only dipped into the water. "Now I know," he cried, "what others have suffered from me, for I burn with love for my own self." Narcissus stared into the pool until he eventually died, fading into the flower that now bears his name—the Narcissus.

Who were the Amazons?

The Amazons were a mythical tribe of female warriors famed for their courage, strength, and skill in battle. They lived at the edge of the Greek world on the coast of the Black Sea. The Amazons discarded or maimed their male children, raising the female children as warriors to maintain their traditions. Several great Greek heroes, including Achilles, Herakles, and Theseus, battled the Amazons during their adventures.

Who was Oedipus?

Oedipus is one of the most tragic figures in Greek mythology. Oedipus's parents, King Laius and Queen Jocasta of Thebes, learned from the Delphic oracle that their next son would grow up to kill his father and marry his mother. Terrified by the prophecy, King Laius pierced the infant's ankles and left him to die on a mountainside. But a kind shepherd found him and took him to Corinth, where he grew up as the adopted son of King Polybus and Queen Merope. They named him Oedipus.

As a young man, Oedipus traveled to the Delphic oracle, where he heard that he would murder his father and marry his mother. Believing that King Polybus and Queen Merope were his true parents, Oedipus fled Corinth and traveled to Thebes. Along the way, Oedipus quarreled with an old man and struck him dead. Although he did not realize it, Oedipus had just killed his true father, King Laius.

Oedipus *means swollen foot.*

What was the Riddle of the Sphinx?

On a road outside the city of Thebes, the Sphinx sat on a rock and watched for travelers, who she challenged with this riddle.

"What has four legs in the morning, two legs at midday, and three legs in the evening?" The correct answer is—a person. (A person crawls on all fours as a baby, walks on two feet as an adult, and needs a cane when old.)

If the traveler could not answer, the Sphinx pounced and devoured them.

Oedipus continued on his way, until he confronted a fierce creature outside Thebes called the Sphinx, a cruel monster with the head and chest of a woman, the body of a lion, and the wings of a bird.

Oedipus answered the Sphinx's riddle, making her so enraged that she flung herself off a cliff. The city of Thebes rejoiced to be rid of the Sphinx. As a reward, Oedipus married Queen Jocasta and became king of Thebes.

How did Oedipus discover his past?

After several years of Oedipus's rule, famine and plague devastated the city of Thebes. The people consulted oracles to find out why and were instructed to find the murderer of King Laius. Determined to save his city, Oedipus relentlessly pursued the identity of the murderer, finally discovering that he himself had killed Laius and that his wife was also his mother. Jocasta hanged herself after learning the truth. Grief-stricken, Oedipus blinded himself, preferring to live in darkness than in the light that showed his sin. Years later, he was banished from Thebes and died in a sacred grove outside Athens.

Who was King Midas?

King Midas was ruler of Phrygia, a land covered with roses. One day, King Midas's servants discovered the satyr Silenus—a creature that was half man, half goat—in a drunken slumber in the king's favorite flower bed. Instead of punishing Silenus, Midas entertained him with food and wine for ten days. The god Dionysus, who considered Silenus a loyal follower, was impressed by this act of generosity. He gave Midas his choice of anything in the world. Before giving the matter much thought, Midas wished that everything he touched would turn to gold. Dionysus knew that the foolish king would soon regret his choice, but the god granted Midas his request anyway.

At first, Midas was delighted with this power. But when he tried to eat, the food turned to gold when it touched his lips. Desperate, Midas went to Dionysus and begged him to return him to normal. Dionysus ordered Midas to bathe in the source of the river Pactolus, where the waters washed his power from him. Today, Greeks believe that gold can be found somewhere in the river's sands.

Midas had another unfortunate encounter with the gods when he was ordered to judge who could play better music: the god Apollo or Pan, a weaker god who dwelled among animal herds in the countryside. Apollo, god of music, played heavenly melodies on a silver lyre. Pan played charming melodies on his reed lute. Midas, who was no expert in music, honestly thought Pan played better. Stupidly, Midas said so. Enraged, Apollo turned Midas's ears into donkey ears. The king was mortified and wore a hat to keep his ears hidden from people. Only one person learned the king's embarrassing secret—his barber, who removed the king's hat to give him a haircut. Although the barber was sworn to secrecy, he was desperate to tell somebody. Finally, the barber dug a hole and whispered: "King Midas has donkey ears!" Satisfied, he covered the hole with dirt, convinced that the secret was safe. Apollo, however, caused weeds to grow on the spot, and when the wind blew through the tall plants, they whispered "King Midas has donkey ears!" Soon, everyone in the land knew the king's humiliating secret.

Who was Daphne?

Daphne, a nymph and daughter of the river god Peneus, loved to hunt in the deep thickets of the forest. She preferred to be alone, and she rejected the offers of love and marriage she received from many young men. One day, the god Apollo noticed Daphne hunting and immediately fell in love. But as he approached her, Daphne grew terrified of the god and ran for her life. Apollo followed swiftly, yelling to her to not be afraid.

Daphne paid no heed, and Apollo chased her until she was only a few feet from his grasp. With Apollo's breath on her shoulder, Daphne screamed to her father for help. As soon as she spoke, her legs snagged into the earth, bark expanded over her skin, and her outstretched arms sprouted leaves. To save her, her father had transformed her into a laurel tree. Apollo, downcast with grief, embraced the tree's trunk and swore that the laurel tree would become his symbol, and that all victors would wear a crown of laurel leaves.

Who was Adonis?

When Adonis was born, he was so beautiful that Aphrodite herself felt the sting of love for him. Determined to keep Adonis for herself, Aphrodite gave the young boy to Persephone to raise away from the world. But Persephone also fell in love with Adonis, and she refused Aphrodite's demands for his return. To make peace between the two goddesses, Zeus ordered Adonis to stay one half of the year with Aphrodite and the other half with Persephone.

While Adonis stayed with Aphrodite, he spent many days in the forest hunting. One day, he cornered a large, wounded boar. Angry and in pain, the boar charged Adonis and lunged his tusk into Adonis's chest. At Adonis's cry, Aphrodite descended from Mount Olympus and found her lover bleeding to death. Even Aphrodite could do nothing to bind the wound, and all the muses and creatures of the world wept. Adonis left the world a gift—wherever his blood dropped, a beautiful crimson anemone flower grew.

How did Arachne offend Athena?

A young woman named Arachne became known throughout Greece for her skillful weaving and embroidering of cloth. As she sat at her loom, she bragged that she had taught herself and owed her talent to no one, not even Athena, goddess of spinners and embroiderers. Suddenly, an old woman appeared at the door and urged Arachne to be more modest. Arrogantly, Arachne stated that she would challenge Athena herself. At these words, the old woman

(continued on page 46)

The Adventures of Odysseus

The story of Odysseus was told by the ancient poet, Homer. His epic poem *The Odyssey* is one of the most important literary works in history.

At the end of the Trojan War, Odysseus and his crew sailed from Troy with the rest of the Greek fleet. According to the story, a storm blew Odysseus's ship off course into an exotic part of the world, full of magic and danger.

Odysseus and his comrades first landed at an island where, after some exploration, they discovered a giant cave. Odysseus and his men were hungry, and they hoped that whoever lived in the cave would give them food and shelter. But Odysseus was horrified when a giant Cyclops returned to the cave, dashed three of his men against the cave wall, and ate them. The others were trapped when the Cyclops rolled a giant boulder across the cave mouth. To escape the deadly Cyclops, Odysseus and his men fashioned a giant stake and rammed it into the Cyclops's single eye as he slept. While the Cyclops bellowed in pain, Odysseus and his men escaped.

Odysseus next landed at another mysterious island. He sent several of his crew inland to explore the island and discover who ruled it. After several days, none of the men had returned. Finally, one man burst from the forest, crying that the rest of the crew had been captured by an evil sorceress, called Circe, who had turned them into wild animals. Odysseus resolved to rescue his men. Aided by the god Hermes, Odysseus was able to enter Circe's palace and force her to free his crew. Circe invited Odysseus to stay in her magical palace, which he did for more than a year.

On ship again, Odysseus sailed past the island of Sirens. The Sirens were hideous creatures with bodies of birds and the heads of women. They could sing so beautifully that sailors jumped from their ships and swam ashore, where the Sirens murdered them for their next meal. Odysseus

had his men block their ears with wax before he strapped himself to the ship's mast so that he could listen to the Sirens' enchanting songs without danger.

Next, Odysseus steered his ship past Scylla and Charybdis, two monsters that lurked on either sides of a strait. Scylla claimed the lives of six crewmen in her jaws. Finally, Odysseus and his crew arrived at Thrinakia, the island of the sun. There, Odysseus's hungry crew ate some cattle from the sun's herds. The sun complained to Zeus, who sent a thunderbolt to shat-

ter Odyssesus's ship as it left the island. Everyone was killed except for Odysseus, who was left stranded on an island with Calypso, a goddess who kept him with her for eight years. Finally, she allowed Odysseus to build a raft and sail back to Penelope in Ithaca.

When Odysseus finally arrived home, he found Penelope and his house besieged by suitors. With the help of his son, Telemachus, Odysseus slaughtered the suitors and once again enjoyed the loving embrace of his faithful wife.

(continued from page 43)

Arachnid, *the scientific name of the spider family, comes from the Greek* Arachne, *which means spider.*

transformed into the goddess Athena. She sat down at a loom and the contest began. Both Arachne and Athena worked in a blur of motion, their hands stitching exquisite cloth. Athena's cloth showed scenes of mortals punished for their lack of respect. In response, Arachne created frank and embarrassing portrayals of the gods—especially Zeus's numerous love affairs. As Arachne and Athena neared completion, Athena looked at the young girl's work. It appeared as beautiful and perfect as her own. Enraged, Athena ripped the cloth from Arachne's loom and beat her on the head with her spinning spool. Distressed and disgraced by this treatment, Arachne hanged herself. Athena felt pity for the proud mortal and sprinkled drops of magic water onto her body, transforming her into a spider that would weave and spin forever.

Who was Sisyphus?

Sisyphus was a brilliant and clever king whose deceptive ways fooled the gods themselves. When Sisyphus angered Zeus, Zeus sent the spirit of death, Thanatos, to bring Sisyphus to the underworld. But Sisyphus had no intention of dying, and he used his trickery to bind Thanatos in chains. Without Thanatos, dead souls could no longer enter the underworld, and Zeus furiously ordered Sisyphus to free him. Naturally, Thanatos turned on Sisyphus as soon as he was unchained. But before Sisyphus died, he secretly told his wife not to bury his body. According to Greek belief, no one could enter the underworld unless they have been properly buried. Waiting to enter the underworld, Sisyphus complained bitterly to Hades about his wife and asked Hades if he could return to life to punish her for not giving him a proper burial. Hades, also angered by Sisyphus's wife, agreed. But once Sisyphus returned to earth, he remained there and lived to a ripe old age.

When Sisyphus finally died as an old man, the gods were determined to give him a task that would leave him no time to scheme or plot. They gave him a boulder to push to the top of a hill. Once he reached the top, he would lose his grip, and the boulder would roll back down to the bottom. Sisyphus had to trudge down the hill and push the boulder again to the top, and he was doomed to repeat the process forever.

Who was Tantalus?

Like Sisyphus, Tantalus drew the wrath of the gods and was punished with perpetual torment. A mortal son of Zeus, Tantalus dined regularly with the gods on Mount Olympus. One day, Tantalus invited the gods to a feast of his own. To test their omniscience, Tantalus decided to kill his own son, Pelops and make him into a stew. When the gods arrived at Tantalus's banquet, they were horrified by the human sacrifice. They resurrected Pelops, who was missing part of his shoulder, which had been eaten by Demeter before she realized what she had been served. The gods fashioned Pelops a new shoulder out of ivory.

As punishment, Zeus banished Tantalus to the underworld, where he forever stood in a pool of water with clusters of fresh fruit hanging overhead. Whenever Tantalus bent down to quench his thirst, the water dried up. Whenever he grasped for fruit to satisfy his hunger, the branch swung out of reach.

The word tantalize, *which means to torment or tease with empty promises, comes from the Greek story of Tantalus.*

Who was Niobe?

Niobe was Tantalus's daughter, and she suffered a punishment even more terrible than her father's. Married to a son of Zeus, Niobe enjoyed wealth and power as queen of the city of Thebes. More than her wealth, she cherished her seven daughters and seven sons, all of them handsome and blessed with intelligence. But because of the number and beauty of her children, Niobe arrogantly began to consider herself greater than the gods. Foolishly, she demanded that the people of Thebes worship her. She ridiculed the goddess Leto, the mother of Apollo and Artemis, for having had only two children, while she had fourteen. Apollo and Artemis heard Niobe's boasts and descended to earth in a fury, with their bows drawn and arrows notched. As Niobe watched in horror, her seven sons and seven daughters were struck down, one by one, in agony. Niobe sank down in grief among their bodies and wept ceaselessly. So she remained, eventually turning into a stone that trickles water forever.

How were the Olympic games started?

A king named Oenomaus had a beautiful daughter, Hippodamia, who attracted the attention of many suitors. But the king jealously guarded his daughter, and he challenged each suitor to a chariot race. If the suitor won, Hippodamia would become his wife. If he lost, the young man sacrificed his life. Oenomaus, however, had a special advantage: his horses were a gift from Ares, the god of war. No suitor could defeat the swift steeds, and soon twelve men died trying to win the princess from her father.

Pelops, Tantalus's son, was returned to life by the gods more handsome than before and was awarded many gifts. One of these was a splendid chariot and four horses from Poseidon. With this gift, Pelops knew he could defeat King Oenomaus and make Hippodamia his wife. When Pelops challenged the king, Hippodamia saw Pelops and fell in love with him. She told the king's stable boy to tamper with Oenomaus's chariot so that Pelops would win the race. The boy did, replacing the wooden pins that held the wheels to the axle with pins of wax.

The next morning, the race began. To Oenomaus's shock, Pelops and his horses galloped neck and neck with his own steeds. Suddenly, the wax pins melted, causing Oenomaus to get tangled in the reins and dragged to his death.

Pelops honored the dead king with a magnificent funeral. As part of the ceremonies, Pelops asked all of Greece to send athletes to compete in contests of strength and skill. Pelops held the games on the plains of Olympia. These games became a tradition and were called the Olympics.

How did the Trojan War begin?

The Trojan War began when the goddess of discord, Eris, was not invited to a wedding. Furious at being snubbed, she cast a golden apple among the wedding guests that bore the words "To the Fairest." The goddesses Aphrodite, Hera, and Athena all wished to have the apple for themselves. Zeus, wanting to avoid this quarrel, ordered a shepherd from the city of Troy to judge which goddess was "the Fairest." His name was Paris.

To persuade Paris that she deserved the apple, each goddess offered him gifts. Hera promised him power and riches. Athena assured him of wisdom and victory in war. Aphrodite offered him the most beautiful woman in the world as his wife. After considering the three offers, Paris decided in favor of Aphrodite.

The most beautiful woman in the world was Helen, Queen of Sparta and wife of King Menelaus. Helped by Aphrodite, Paris seduced Helen and took her back to Troy. Enraged, King Menelaus called on the other Greek leaders, who were bound by oath to help Menelaus retrieve his wife. Soon, several thousand ships darkened the waters around Greece. Filled with soldiers eager for adventure and plunder, the armada set sail for the walled city of Troy. The Trojan War had begun.

Who was Achilles?

Achilles was the greatest Greek warrior to fight at Troy. When Achilles was an infant, his mother held him by the ankle and dipped him into the River Styx, a river that separated the world of the living from the underworld. The magical water made him invulnerable except for the one part of him that stayed dry—his heel. Achilles joined King Menelaus before the walls of Troy when the war began. After ten years of combat, Achilles quarreled with Menelaus's brother, King Agamemnon, and refused to fight any longer.

Without their greatest warrior, the Greeks were driven back with heavy losses. Seeing that they were near defeat, Achilles' best friend, Patroclus, took Achilles' armor and entered the battle. At first, the Trojans believed he was Achilles, and they retreated. But Troy's greatest warrior, Hector, killed Patroclus and took the armor.

Achilles was plunged into grief when he heard the news of his friend's death, and he reappeared on the battlefield, eager for revenge. Dressed in new armor provided by the gods, Achilles drove the Trojans back into their city, slaughtering them by the dozens. Finally, Achilles chased Hector around the walls three times before striking him down.

But even Achilles did not survive the Trojan war. After dipping an arrow in poison, Paris skillfully aimed his bow and launched the shaft into Achilles' one weak spot—his heel. Today, we use the phrase "Achilles heel" to describe a vulnerable spot.

What was the Trojan horse?

By the time of Achilles' death, the Trojan War had lasted more than ten years, and the weary Greeks were eager to go home. The Greek warrior Odysseus devised one last scheme to enter and defeat Troy.

As a trick, the Greeks boarded their ships and sailed away, leaving a giant wooden horse on the beach. The Trojans were delighted to find the Greeks gone, and they took the wooden horse within the walls of their city as a tribute to the gods. Unknown to them, Odysseus and several dozen Greek warriors were hidden inside. When night fell and the city was asleep, the Greeks stole out of the horse and opened the city gates. Thousands of Greek soldiers who had returned in their ships under the cover of darkness, rushed through the open gates. The surprise was complete. Greek warriors swarmed through the city, looting and burning buildings and slaughtering the confused, desperate Trojan soldiers.

What happened after the fall of Troy?

For the Greeks, the Trojan War was a hollow victory. The gods grew angry with the Greeks for destroying holy temples while sacking Troy. Few of the Greek warriors survived the journey home, and those who did found their kingdoms changed and overrun with revolt, treachery, and general disorder. King Menelaus forgave Helen and took her back to Sparta, where she again ruled as queen. Odysseus wandered for ten years before he finally returned to his beloved wife, Penelope, in Ithaca.

ROME

Who were the ancient Romans?

According to legend, the city of Rome was founded in 753 B.C. Through the next several centuries, the Romans expanded their power by conquering neighboring cities

Greek Gods and their Roman Equivalents

The Romans matched Greek gods and their stories with their own gods. Some Greek gods—Apollo, for example—had no Roman equivalents, so the Romans incorporated them into their mythology without changing their names.

Greek	Roman
Cronos	Saturn
Zeus	Jupiter, or Jove
Hera	Juno
Poseidon	Neptune
Hades	Pluto, or Dis

Greek	Roman
Ares	Mars
Athena	Minerva
Aphrodite	Venus
Apollo	Apollo
Hermes	Mercury
Demeter	Ceres
Artemis	Diana
Hephaistos	Vulcan
Hestia	Vesta
Dionysus	Bacchus, or Liber
Eros	Cupid
Pan	Faunus

and territories. By the second century A.D., the Romans had created one of the greatest empires the world had ever seen, stretching from Egypt to the hills of Scotland. In 476 A.D., the city of Rome fell to invading barbarians, ending Roman authority over western Europe.

What kind of myths did the Romans tell?

Compared to the myths created by the rich imagination of the Greeks, the Roman myths can appear dull. The Romans themselves recognized this. After conquering Greece in 133 B.C., the Romans adopted many of the Greek gods and their stories and changed the Greek names into Roman ones. For example, Poseidon, the Greek god of the sea, was called Neptune by the Romans. Romans worshipped a number of smaller gods of their own. But the Roman gods rarely have personalities or appear in myths.

Roman myths showed more originality when they described the origins of the magnificent Roman Empire. Many Roman myths tell about the founding of the city of Rome. Other myths honored the exploits of the Roman army and its generals. Still other myths taught young Romans to be patriotic and serve their city with courage and honor.

How was Rome founded?

Two great myths explain the founding of Rome. The first myth explains how Aeneas founded the Roman civilization. Aeneas, the greatest of Roman heroes, originally fought the Greeks at the city of Troy. When the Greeks ravaged Troy, Aeneas was guided by his mother—the goddess Venus—and escaped with a small band of followers. Although despairing at the loss of his city and his loved ones, Aeneas answered the call of duty to establish a great civilization on the Italian peninsula.

The second myth begins in the city of Alba Longa in Italy, which was founded by Aeneas's son, Ascanius. King Numitor, ruler of Alba Longa, was forced from his throne by his younger brother, Amulius. Amulius did not want Numitor's daughter, Rhea Silvia, to produce any heirs who might later threaten his rule. He forced her to become a vestal virgin, thus preventing her from having any children. But the Roman war god, Mars, seduced Rhea Silvia

The infants Romulus and Remus, the mythical founders of Rome, suckle the milk from the she-wolf. Romans used the image as a symbol of their power. This cast bronze is among the most well known depictions of the myth.

and left her pregnant with twin sons. After Amulius discovered the pregnancy, he imprisoned Rhea Silvia and later left her two newborn infants on a river bank to die. A she-wolf discovered the wailing babies and suckled them as if they were wolf cubs, until a shepherd, named Faustulus, took them and raised them as his own children.

The two boys, called Romulus and Remus, grew into powerful warriors who robbed shepherds. During one raid, Remus was captured and brought before Amulius. While Remus sat in prison, Faustulus explained to Romulus the circumstances of his birth. When Faustulus finished his story, Romulus rescued Remus, murdered Amulius, and restored his father Numitor as king.

The two brothers then decided to leave Alba Longa to build their own city. They returned to the spot where the she-wolf had discovered them on the riverbank and began digging trenches to set boundaries for the new city. But the ambitious brothers grew jealous of each other, and they quarreled over the exact location of the border. Remus jumped over Romulus's boundary trench to mock its ability as a line of defense. Infuriated, Romulus struck Remus down and named the new city after himself— Rome. Romulus became the new city's first ruler, and he established fair laws and customs.

Who was Pygmalion?

Pygmalion was a young and handsome sculptor who despised women. One day, Pygmalion began carving a beautiful woman from a block of stone. He labored for days on the statue, delicately chipping away stone and brushing away dust. The statue appeared so lovely that no woman alive could rival its beauty. Pygmalion became obsessed with the statue, placing gifts before it and lying it next to him in his bed at night.

But the statue remained a cold and unresponsive stone, and Pygmalion was filled with despair.

The goddess of love, Venus, noticed Pygmalion's passion. On the goddess' holiday, Pygmalion came to her temple and pleaded for a woman to marry as beautiful as the woman he had created from stone. Venus answered his prayer. When he returned to his studio, the statue's skin

The Adventures of Aeneas

The adventures of Aeneas are told by the Roman poet Virgil in his epic, *The Aeneid*. Virgil borrowed elements of his tale from the Greek epics *The Iliad* and *The Odyssey*. The story begins with the fall of Troy, when Aeneas and his comrades fled the burning city in their ships. The god Apollo sent Aeneas a dream vision, that told him of a future home on the western coast of Italy.

Juno, who hated the Trojans because Paris had picked Venus instead of her, sent a storm that blew Aeneas and his men to the coast of northern Africa. There, Aeneas met and fell in love with the beautiful Queen Dido, the ruler of Carthage. Venus sent her son, Cupid, to make Dido love Aeneas and thus keep him safe. The two lovers shared a passionate relationship, and soon Aeneas forgot about Italy. But Jupiter sent Mercury to remind Aeneas of his sacred destiny and to leave Carthage. Tragically, Aeneas left, causing Dido to commit suicide. Her funeral pyre burned brightly on the horizon as Aeneas and his men sailed away.

When Aeneas landed on the western coast of Italy, a prophet told him that he must wage war and take a bride. Aeneas and his men sailed up the Tiber river to the site of the future city. Aeneas then turned his attention to Lavinia, the daughter of a local ruler, King Latinus. Latinus warmly welcomed Aeneas, but his wife, Queen Amata, wanted Lavinia to marry another man, Turnus.

Turnus grew ferociously jealous of Aeneas, and soon the Trojans and Turnus's army were at war. While Aeneas was away seeking allies, Turnus and his men attacked the Trojan camp. The Trojans fought and survived several disasters until Aeneas returned with thirty boats filled with soldiers. Armed with sacred armor given to him by Venus, Aeneas met Turnus in single combat before the two armies. After several hours of fierce fighting, Aeneas killed Turnus with a mighty stroke of his sword.

The victor, Aeneas married Lavinia and established the city of Lavinium. Aeneas's son, Ascanius, would found another city—Alba Longa.

grew warm, her hair tumbled down her shoulders, and she stepped down from the pedestal a living, breathing woman. Pygmalion rushed to embrace her, thanking Venus for this gift of love.

Who were Cupid and Psyche?

Psyche was a princess so beautiful that people began to honor her instead of Venus. Furious at the young princess,

Venus told her son, Cupid, to make Psyche fall in love with the ugliest creature on earth. But when Cupid glimpsed Psyche, he himself fell in love. While Venus waited impatiently, Cupid used his power to prevent anyone from loving Psyche. Psyche's parents were disturbed, and they asked the Apollo oracle for help. The oracle responded that Psyche must be left on a mountain top to wait for her husband, a horrible dragon.

But this was all part of Cupid's plan. When the weeping princess was left alone, he swept down and took her to his palace made from gold, silver, and gems. Cupid made Psyche promise never to look at him. Psyche was so delighted with her new home, she agreed. Whenever she

This statue of the goddess Venus is a Roman copy of the famous Cnidian Venus statue, much admired and often imitated by the Romans.

felt lonely, Cupid whispered gently in her ear. Although Psyche never saw Cupid since he only came to her at night, they became lovers and married.

When Psyche's sisters visited her, they grew jealous of her splendid surroundings. They wondered, who was this husband? From Psyche's confused answers, they realized that she had never set eyes upon him. Driven by their own envy, the sisters convinced Psyche that her husband must be a monster. They gave her an oil lamp and a knife to kill him. That night, Psyche put the dagger in one hand and the oil lamp in the other. While Cupid slept beside her, she shined the light on his face. To her shock, Cupid was not a monster, but a god of incredible beauty. She suddenly dropped the knife and the oil lamp, spilling the burning oil onto Cupid's shoulder. He woke and realized immediately what had happened. Heartbroken and betrayed, he told Psyche that love could not exist where there was no trust. Then, he disappeared.

How did Psyche recover Cupid's love?

Shattered by her loss, Psyche was determined to recover her husband's love. After prayer, she realized that she would have to humbly serve Venus, the goddess who had hated her so passionately. First, Venus taunted Psyche and ordered her to complete an impossible task. Venus piled together millions of various types of tiny seeds and told Psyche to sort them into separate containers in one night. As Psyche despaired, some ants took pity on her and sorted the seeds. Surprised and angered at this result, Venus next ordered Psyche to recover strands of golden fleece from fierce sheep. As Psyche approached the flock, a reed in a stream advised Psyche to wait until nightfall. When the sheep would pass through thick thornbushes, the thorns would catch and gather the fleece. Delighted, Psyche followed this advice and collected the golden fleece from the bushes. For the final task, Venus told Psyche to travel to the underworld and return with some of Proserpina's (the goddess of death) beauty in a box. Psyche obediently set out and met a man in a tower who told her exactly how to approach the gates of the underworld. Proserpina readily gave Psyche the box and soon she was hurrying back to the land of the living. But Psyche was suddenly seized with curiosity and cracked open the box to glimpse inside. She immediately fainted and fell into a deathlike state.

Meanwhile, Cupid had recovered from the oil burn and his anger and longed to see his wife again. When he found Psyche, he woke her and brought her back to Olympus. There, Jupiter ordered Venus to end her hostility to Psyche and the two lovers were married again in the sight of the gods.

INDIA

Where do the myths of India come from?

Indian mythology comes from a complex mix of stories and religion that originated thousands of years ago. The first Indian myths describe the Vedic gods. These gods usually represent the forces of nature—fire, wind, and rain. Their champion was Indra. Over time, Indra and the Vedic gods were transformed or replaced by gods of the Hindu religion.

Who was Indra?

The leader of the ancient Vedic gods, Indra rode across the sky in a golden chariot and threw thunderbolts with deadly accuracy. A priest, Tvashtri, hated Indra, and he created a three-headed son to seize Indra's throne. When Tvashtri's son challenged Indra, Indra killed him with a thunderbolt and cut off his three heads. Enraged, Tvashtri created a giant dragon called Vritra to avenge his son's death. Vritra flew through the heavens and swallowed Indra in one gulp. But Indra tickled the monster's throat and was coughed out. Vritra and Indra clashed for several hours before Indra fled before the dragon's superior strength. Later, Indra and Vritra agreed to a truce, even though Indra continued to look for ways to kill Vritra.

In this bronze sculpture from the 12th century Chola dynasty, four-armed Shiva is shown as Natarja, the lord of the dance and the source of all movement in the universe. This is a typical representation of Shiva dancing inside a ring of fire.

Finally, in the darkness of twilight, he smashed a column onto Vritra's head and killed him instantly. With Vritra dead, the forces of chaos were banished from the universe. Indra separated the water from land and created the sun. Indra became the lord of all gods and creatures on earth.

How did Indra reward loyalty?

One day, a hungry hawk chased a pigeon through the air. A ruler called King Vrishadarbha noticed the poor pigeon and offered it protection in his palace. The hawk followed the pigeon and landed next to the king. The hawk explained to the king that he was hungry and needed to eat the pigeon to survive. But the king had made a vow to protect the pigeon, and he would not break it. He told the hawk to eat something else—a frog, a mouse, or some other animal. Impatient, the hawk asked the king for some of his own flesh. Amazingly, the king began cutting pieces from his own body. He planned to stop when the amount equaled the weight of the pigeon. But when the king's flesh was put on a scale, the pigeon always weighed more. The king continued to cut until he was little more than a skeleton. Watching from heaven, the gods admired the king's loyalty to the bird. They restored the king to his former health and invited him to live with them—a reward for those who are loyal.

How did Indra reward friendship?

A wise man called Gautama lived alone in the forest. One day, he discovered a baby elephant wandering alone. Gautama took the elephant into his home and protected it. Over the years, Gautama cherished the elephant as it grew strong and powerful. The handsome animal drew the

Hindu Gods

The Hindu gods replaced the Vedic gods in India. Today, Hinduism is one of the most prominent religions in the world, with more than 700 million followers. The three great gods of Hinduism —Brahma, Vishnu, and Shiva—are called the Trimurti.

Brahma is the personified form of Brahman as a male god. Brahman can be described as the force or spiritual energy behind everything in the universe. Brahma emerged from the original chaos and created the universe. He is portrayed with four faces and four arms.

Vishnu, also known as the protector, is a major Hindu god and preserver of the world. Kind and generous, Vishnu descends to the earth when evil threatens to overcome the forces of good. He appears as a form called an avatar. Two his most recognized avatars are Krishna and Rama. Vishnu is married to Shri, goddess of prosperity and fortune.

The third god of the Trimurti is Shiva, who has been called both destroyer and creator. Shiva controls the movement of the universe through his dancing (he is often portrayed as a statue dancing within a ring of fire). He has four arms and a third eye in his forehead, which both illuminates and destroys.

Devi is a Hindu goddess with many names and powers. As Parvati, she is Shiva's wife. As Durga, she is a champion warrior who ruthlessly destroys the demons who threaten the stability of the earth. When enraged, she becomes the terrifying Kali.

The goddess Kali represents the forces of destruction (her name means the dark one). With her four arms she carries a sword, a severed head, a holy book, and a string of prayer beads. Around her neck she wears a necklace of skulls.

Ganesha is the elephant-headed son of Parvati and Shiva and the popular god of prosperity and good fortune.

The twelve-armed goddess Devi is pictured here as Durga, slaying the menacing Mahishasura.

attention of a king. He came to Gautama and demanded the elephant for himself. Through his tears, Gautama begged the king not to take it. The elephant, he explained, was not his possession, but his dearest friend. The king then offered a treasure of jewels and gold for the elephant. Again, Gautama refused. The king then asked, "What if I asked Brahma, the creator, and he told me the elephant was mine?" Gautama answered that his love for the elephant was greater than any wealth—Brahma would certainly recognize that.

Delighted with these answers, the king revealed himself as the god Indra. He told Gautama that he could have anything he wished. Gautama did not wish for wealth or knowledge, he only asked to remain with his elephant. Indra was not surprised by Guatama's answer. Gautama already had wisdom, and he who knows the value of a friend is already rich.

What is the Hindu myth of creation?

The Hindus believe that the universe creates and destroys itself in an endless cycle. In the beginning of the creation cycle, the god Brahma contains all things within himself. First, he creates the elements—water, fire, wind, sky, and earth. Upon the earth, Brahma brings forth rocks, mountains, and oceans. He organizes time and fashions the gods, demons, and people. Brahma then uses his own body to create night and day. From a second body, Brahma brings forth animals—horses from his feet, goats from his mouth, cows from his stomach, sheep from his chest, and all the rest of the animals in the world. The strands of his hair become trees and vegetation.

The Avatars of Vishnu

As the protector of the world, Vishnu has appeared nine times (so far) to save humankind from evil and disaster. These appearances on earth in human form are called avatars.

Vishnu first appeared as the fish Matsya to rescue the first man, Manu. Matsya warned Manu that a giant flood would cover the earth. Following Matsya's directions, Manu built a boat and filled it with provisions. Later, when the flood waters surged around the boat, Matsya towed it to safety.

The second avatar was Kurma, a tortoise. He supported the earth while the gods churned the ocean in search of immortality.

Varaha, the boar, was the third avatar. When the earth fell into the ocean, he raised it on his tusk, saving it from destruction.

To become the fourth avatar, Vishnu changed himself into the monster Narasimha, half-lion and half-man. He fought and killed the terrible demon, Hiranyakashipu.

Vamana, the fifth avatar, was a small dwarf. The demon Bali led an army that conquered the world. Vamana appeared before Bali and begged him for as much land as he could cover with three strides. When Bali agreed, Vamana transformed himself into a giant and stepped across the world with three tremendous strides. The world was saved.

The sixth avatar was a priest named Parasurama. He attacked and killed Arjuna, a hundred-armed warrior.

Rama and Krishna are the seventh and eighth avatars and are major figures in Hindu myths. Rama traveled on an epic quest to recover his lost wife and kingdom. Krishna killed several monsters that threatened to destroy the world.

The ninth avatar is Buddha, who tricks sinners into being punished.

Kalkin, the tenth avatar, has not yet appeared. He will come as a warrior on a white horse and establish a new era of peace and prosperity.

An 18th-century Indian painting shows Vishnu in the center, surrounded by his ten different avatars in the surrounding panels. From right to left: 1) Matsya the fish 2) Kurma the tortoise 3) Varaha the boar 4) Narasimha the man-lion 5) Vamana the dwarf 6) Rama 7) Krishna 8) Parashurama the brahman 9) Buddha 10) Kalkin, who will appear on a white horse (in some versions of the myth he is the horse).

Who was the kindest god?

Bhrigu, an Indian wise man, wondered which god—Brahma, Shiva, or Vishnu—was greatest. To find out, he visited Brahma and did not pay proper respect. Brahma bristled with anger but accepted Bhrigu's apologies. Next, Bhrigu visited Shiva and snubbed him. Shiva rose up in rage and prepared to destroy Bhrigu. He only calmed down after Bhrigu apologized repeatedly. Finally, Bhrigu visited Vishnu, who was sleeping on the floor. Bhrigu kicked Vishnu in the chest. Vishnu woke up and grabbed Bhrigu's foot. He asked Bhrigu if he had hurt his foot and began massaging it. Stunned by this act of kindness, Bhrigu proclaimed Vishnu the god most worthy of worship.

Who was Rama?

Rama was one of the most famous avatars of Vishnu. His story is told in the massive Indian epic *Ramayana*.

The son of a king, Rama grew into a handsome and powerful young warrior. He proved his strength in the foreign court of King Janaka. The king owned a bow once used by the god Shiva that was so large that no one could even lift or bend it. Rama hefted the tremendous weapon and pulled it back until it snapped in two. Impressed by Rama's display of power, King Janaka gave Rama his beautiful daughter, Sita, in marriage. Rama returned to his kingdom, but his evil stepmother created a plot that banished Rama and his new wife to the wild jungles outside the palace.

How did Ravana capture Sita?

Rama, Sita, and Rama's brother, Lakshman, wandered into the jungle, which was filled with treacherous magicians called Rakshas. A Raksha woman fell in love with Rama, but Rama rejected her advances, and the woman attacked Sita in rage. Lakshman knocked the woman to the ground and cut off her nose. Howling with pain and humiliation, the Raksha woman went to her brother Ravana, the ruler of the Rakshas. For revenge, Ravana planned to kidnap Sita. Ravana magically turned a Raksha into a beautiful deer. Despite Rama and Lakshman's warnings, Sita saw the beautiful deer and wanted it for herself. Finally, Rama tracked the deer through the jungle and shot it. As the deer collapsed, it cried out in an imitation of Rama's voice. Sita heard the cry and urged Lakshman to find out if Rama was injured. Lakshman suspected treachery, but he finally left. With Sita now alone, Ravana appeared and took her away in his flying chariot.

How did Rama rescue Sita?

While Rama and Lakshman desperately searched for Sita, they met a monkey-king. Weeping, the monkey-king told them that his evil brother had wrongfully seized his throne. He promised to help Rama and Lakshman find Sita if they helped him recover his kingdom. Agreeing to the plan, Rama and Lakshman killed the evil brother. In gratitude, the monkey-king ordered his monkeys to travel all over India in search of Sita. They finally found her imprisoned with Ravana on the distant island of Ceylon, known as Sri Lanka today.

Rama traveled to the coast and demanded that Ocean grant him passage to the island. After Rama angrily launched several arrows into the sea, Ocean told him to seek the aid of the god Nala. Nala, a skilled builder, directed the monkeys to construct a bridge of trees and boulders to the island. When the bridge was completed after only five days, Rama led an army of monkeys into battle against the Rakshas. For days, the armies clashed in bloody warfare. The powerful Rakshas were slain until only Ravana himself remained alive. Rama and Ravana dueled for days. Finally, Rama launched a holy arrow into Ravana's body, killing him.

How did Sita and Rama reunite?

When Sita was freed at last, Rama coldly ignored her because he suspected her virtue was tainted. In despair at the rejection, Sita built a funeral pyre and stepped into the roaring flames. The flames, however, did not harm her flesh or burn her clothes, proving her purity. At this sign of his wife's virtue, Rama embraced her, and the couple returned to rule their kingdom for a thousand years.

How did Shiva form his third eye?

Shiva had several squabbles with his wife, Parvati. On one occasion, Parvati playfully snuck up behind Shiva and covered his eyes with her hands. Suddenly, the world was covered in darkness. Enraged, Shiva created a third eye in his forehead.

Why did Ganesha have an elephant head?

The goddess Parvati was sad because she had no children. When she asked her husband, Shiva, for a child, he refused. The response only made Parvati more lonesome and depressed. When Shiva observed her sadness, he bound together cloth from a dress and handed it to Parvati. Parvati looked down at the bundle and saw the face of a baby boy peeking back at her. Overjoyed, Parvati devoted herself to raising the new child. At first, Shiva was delighted with his wife's attention to the baby. Over time, however, he grew jealous. One day, he turned in rage towards the boy, his third eye sweeping across the baby's head and burning it away. As Parvati screamed in grief, Shiva hastily looked for a way to repair his mistake. An elephant stood nearby, and Shiva cut off its head and placed it on the infant's body. Restored, the boy grew into the kind elephant-headed god, Ganesha.

The Indians revere the elephant for its strength and intelligence. They employ it as a symbol of happiness and wisdom.

Where did disease come from?

On one occasion, the gods of India gathered to make sacrifices, but one god was left out—Shiva. Encouraged by his wife, Shiva became furious for being uninvited. He descended upon the other gods in a terrifying roar. Shiva's rage focused into a single drop of sweat on his forehead, which fell to the earth and exploded into fire. A hairy monster with red eyes jumped from the flames and spread misery through the world. This monster was disease personified. The god Brahma promised Shiva that he would be included at all future sacrifices and begged him to stop the monster. But instead of completely destroying disease, Shiva broke it into smaller ailments—headaches, hiccups, blindness, colds, and fevers. These ailments still plague people today.

How will the world end?

The Hindus believe that the earth is born, exists, and is then destroyed in an endless cycle. Brahma gives birth to the world, Vishnu protects it, and Shiva destroys it. When it

Ganesha, the kind elephant-headed god, is shown in a brightly colored statuette made in the 1700s. Such figures are still widely popular in Indian culture.

is time for the world to come to an end, a one-hundred-year drought will kill many of the world's creatures. Vishnu will then transform into the god Rudra and enter the sun. The sun will increase in heat until all the water on earth will steam, boil, and dry up. The earth will then be cleansed in fire. Then Shiva as the god Rudra will blow great clouds together, and sheets of rain will swamp the earth for one thousand years. With the universe in a state of watery chaos, Brahma will create the new world.

CHINA

When was Chinese mythology created?

Records of Chinese mythology can be traced back to 2000 B.C., though the stories were told long before then. The

Chinese worshipped a number of different gods in the form of mountains, trees, rivers, clouds, the sun, and the moon. Over time, the Chinese also prayed to their ancestors. Today, Chinese mythology comes from the ancient gods and three major systems of belief—Taoism, Confucianism, and Buddhism.

What is the Chinese myth of creation?

In the beginning, the universe was a chaotic swirl of elements in the shape of an egg. Inside the egg shape, the elements formed two opposites: the Yin and Yang. The Yin (the female principle) and Yang (the male principle) gave birth to a god, Pan Gu. The egg ruptured and split open. The lighter elements, Yang, floated to the top, while the heavier ones, Yin, sank to the bottom. Between them lay Pan Gu, who began to grow. Everyday, for eighteen thousand years, Pan Gu grew ten feet. As he became taller, he lifted the lighter part of the elements and created heaven. The heavier parts remained beneath his feet and became the earth.

Weary after so much labor, Pan Gu died. His breath became the wind and clouds. His voice echoed as rumbles of thunder. His flesh became the fields and ground, and the trees and grass were his hair. His left eye climbed into the sky as the sun, and his right eye glistened at night as the moon. His blood flooded into rivers, lakes, and the ocean. His teeth and bones splintered into metal and rock. Priceless jewels were formed from the marrow within his bones. His sweat fell out of the sky as rain and dew. The fleas and bugs that lived on his body became animals and people.

How did Nu Gua create people?

In this creation myth, the Chinese goddess Nu Gua created the first people. After the creation of the world, the goddess Nu Gua lived on earth, lonely and sad. One day, after glimpsing her reflection in a pool, she had an idea. She scooped up a handful of yellow mud and molded a copy of herself. She worked long and hard, creating a small number of people and breathed life into them. To work more quickly, she dragged a cord through mud and flicked

Taoism, Confucianism, and Buddhism

Taoism originated in China in the third century B.C. Taoism taught that individuals should seek to understand the basic structure of the universe—called the Tao—instead of worrying about what society dictated. Taoism urged people to return to the simplicity of farm life and seek to live in harmony with nature, not to dominate it.

Confucianism was a way of life founded by the philosopher Confucius around 500 B.C. Confucius taught his followers to respect and cherish relationships, especially within the family. He set standards for rulers in conduct and behavior and champi-oned education. Confucianism heavily influenced almost every aspect of Chinese life.

Buddhism began with the teachings of Siddhartha Gautama, who became the Buddha (or the enlightened one) in India in the sixth century B.C. The Buddha taught his followers to reject earthly desires and possessions. By renouncing worldly pleasures, people could escape the painful cycle of life and death and enter a state of perfection—nirvana. The Buddha's teachings spread to China in the first century A.D. and strongly influenced Chinese religion and culture.

pieces of earth onto the ground. These pieces sprang up as humans. They wandered off and settled in the hills and fields. Although she rarely saw her people, Nu Gua often heard their voices and never felt lonely again.

How did Nu Gua save the people?

A vicious quarrel once broke out between the water god, Gong Gong, and the fire god, Zhu Rong. The fire god ruled the universe, using his power to make sure the sun set and rose properly. Nu Gua's people on earth prospered under the Zhu Rong's rule. The water god, however, grew jealous of the fire god, and he gathered together an army of sea creatures to conquer the universe. When he saw this challenge, Zhu Rong unleashed blazing heat that dried up the rivers and burned the sea creatures into submission. Gong Gong toppled a mountain that held up one corner of heaven. A giant hole appeared in the northwest sky, throwing the universe out of balance and causing a huge pit to form in the south-

Pan Gu, creator of the world, is shown holding the Yin and Yang symbol in this 19th-century Chinese lithograph. Yin represented shadow, darkness, and feminine characteristics. Yang meant sunshine or light and embodied masculine characteristics. Yin and Yang often symbolized contrasting pairs in the universe—life and death, good and evil, male and female. In Chinese philosophy, Yin and Yang were seen as mutually dependent and equally important.

eastern corner of the world. Heaven and earth fell into chaos as the water of the world rushed southeast toward the pit. Floods and droughts ravaged the countryside. To save her people from the disasters, Nu Gua melted stones in a furnace and plugged the hole in heaven. She then killed a tortoise and used its four legs to prop up heaven, ensuring that this disaster could never happen again.

What is the Chinese flood myth?

One day, a farmer in his field noticed the distant rumble of thunder. As the first drops of rain fell, the man returned to his house and hoisted a giant iron cage outside his door. The storm soon blew around the house, and tor-

Cosmic Disasters

Every society on earth has suffered from a natural disaster—floods, fires, volcanoes, tidal waves, drought. People told myths to explain why these disasters occurred. In Chinese, Greek, American Indian, and Babylonian mythologies, a massive flood almost destroys mankind. In Japan, a myth describes how the sun stopped shining—which may have been inspired by an eclipse or an especially cold winter.

rents of rain crashed against the roof. Through the tumbling clouds and lightning, the man glimpsed the Thunder God himself. Before the god could react, the cunning farmer speared him with a fork and slammed him into the cage. Immediately, the storm disappeared. The next morning, the farmer went to the market. Before he left, he strictly warned his two children not to give the god any water. But after the man was gone, the god begged and cried for a drink. The kind children heard his pleas and gave him a small sip of water. Suddenly, the god swelled in size and exploded from the cage. To repay the children's kindness, the god pulled a tooth from his mouth and told them to plant it. The children obeyed his order and a giant gourd sprang from the ground. Soon after, clouds formed and rain began drenching the earth. The farmer returned from the market and told his children to climb into the gourd while he built a boat. As the rivers and oceans began to rise around them, the farmer climbed into his ship and floated next to the gourd. Soon, everything on earth was covered with water. The waters continued to rise until the farmer and his children neared heaven itself. They cried out to the Lord of Heaven to end the flood. Hearing their pleas, the Lord of Heaven ordered the Water God to push back the waters. The Water God obeyed, but he did it so quickly that the farmer's boat crashed to the ground, killing him. His two children were the only survivors.

How did Nu Gua restore humanity?

Saddened by the destruction of her people, Nu Gua gave birth to a ball of flesh. The gods sliced the ball into tiny pieces and carried them into heaven. There, a gust of

Throughout the Han dynasty, the Chinese creation goddess, Nu Gua, was said to be married to the god Fu Xi. The couple were portrayed with human heads and entwined serpentine tails.

wind scattered the pieces all over the world. As each piece landed on earth, a person sprang up, filling the world again with people.

How did Yi save the world?

A long time ago, there were ten suns that lived together in a tree beyond the eastern horizon. Every day, the goddess Xi He took one sun in her chariot and galloped across the sky, returning the sun to the tree at dusk. Each sun had one turn every ten days. But the suns grew tired of this arrangement. They wanted to be in the sky all the time. One day, they burst from the tree and appeared in the sky together. At first, the people on earth were delighted by the extra warmth and light provided by the ten suns. But then drought came, and the rivers and oceans began drying up. The ruler on earth, Yao, prayed to heaven for help. The Lord of Heaven heard the prayers and ordered the suns to return to their tree. But the suns were enjoying themselves immensely, and they had no intention of leaving their places in the sky. Finally, the Lord of Heaven sent Yi, an expert archer, to scare them. Yi strung his magical bow and launched an arrow at the nearest sun. The arrow struck its target and a dead crow—the spirit of the sun—plunged out of the sky. But the other suns hardly noticed, and Yi was forced to shoot all of the suns out of the sky except for one. With one sun, the climate returned to normal, and Yi was worshipped as a hero.

How was the silkworm created?

Once, long ago, a man left his house to conduct business. His daughter missed him terribly. While grooming a stallion, she whispered to herself that she would marry anyone who brought her father home. Instantly, the stallion bolted off. Several miles away, the man was surprised when the stallion galloped up and begged him to sit on his back. Alarmed, the man jumped on the stallion and was carried home. When he discovered nothing was wrong, the daughter explained that the horse simply must have understood how much she missed her father. The father, overjoyed to be home, rewarded the stallion with extra food. But the stallion appeared depressed and refused to eat it. Finally, the daughter remembered her words about marriage and told her father. Enraged that a horse would dare think of marrying his daughter, the father slaughtered the horse and laid its skin out in the sun. When the daughter came near the skin, it leaped up, wrapped around her, and flew away. Her father chased the skin and finally found it at the top of a tree. His daughter was still inside, but she had been transformed into a creature like a caterpillar. Her head, which now looked like a horse's head, bobbed back and forth, releasing a fine white thread. The thread—silk— amazed everyone with its strength and beauty. Later, it was woven into the clothing of emperors.

How did old man Yu move mountains?

An old man called Yu lived in the shadow of two enormous mountains. Everyday, Yu had to detour around the mountains in order to walk to the village. Finally, at the age of eighty, he grew so weary with the trip that he decided to move the mountains out of the way. Yu gathered his three sons and many grandsons together and told them of his scheme. They thought it was a great idea, but Yu's wife laughed at him. "You can't even move two piles of cow dung," she mocked. "And where are you going to put the rocks and earth you remove from the mountain?" Yu thought about this for a while and said, "We'll dump it in the ocean!"

After a year of hard work, Yu, his sons, and his grandsons, piled rocks and dirt from the mountain into carts and hauled it to the ocean. Along the way, they met a wise man who lived along a river. He ridiculed Yu. "How do you think you can move two mountains?" he said with scorn. "You're just an old man who is nearer to the grave everyday."

"You think you are a wise man," said Yu, "but you are lacking in vision. In time, my grandsons will have children who will in turn also have children. Some day, my dream to remove those mountains will become a reality. As each day passes, the realization of my dream can only increase, as these two mountains can only decrease."

A god heard the old man's story and was moved by his determination. He ordered two gods to carry the mountains on their back and place one east of Shuo and the other south of Yong. The old man's dream had come true.

JAPAN

Where did Japanese mythology come from?

The primary religion in Japan is called Shinto, and the Shinto religion's gods and spirits are the main characters in Japanese mythology. We know most of these stories because in A.D. 711, a Japanese empress ordered her servant, Ono Yasumoro, to write these tales in a collection called the *Kojiki*, or Record of Ancient Matters.

What is the Japanese myth of creation?

The world began as a formless mass that drifted aimlessly like a jellyfish in water. Out of this mass, a slender reed arose. This was Kuntiokotachi—the first god. Two more gods joined him, and together they created seven generations of gods and goddesses—ending with the male Izanagi and female Izanami. The gods ordered the couple to create order in the world. Standing on the Bridge of Heaven, which spanned across the watery void, Izanagi stirred the depths with a jeweled spear. When he pulled the spear from the water, the drops became an island called Onokoro. Onokoro was the first solid land.

Together, Izanagi and Izanami built a palace on Onokoro, with a central stone pillar. Izanagi walked one way around the pillar while Izanami walked in the opposite direction. When they met together face to face, they carried out the courtship of marriage. Soon afterwards, Izanami gave birth to a son. They discovered to their horror that the baby was deformed, and they named him Hiruko (meaning *Leech-Child*). They placed him a reed boat and set him adrift. Hiruko became the god of fisherman. The next time Izanami gave birth, she had healthy children—the eight islands of Japan and numerous gods and goddesses, including the gods of trees, mountains, and wind. When Izanami gave birth to the god of fire, Kagusutchi, she was so badly burned that she died.

How did Izanagi try to resurrect his wife?

Enraged at his wife's death, Izanagi cut off Kagusutchi's head. Still, this act did little to ease his grief. Desperate, Izanagi went searching for Izanami in Yomi, the world of darkness where spirits dwell. Izanami appeared at the entrance to Yomi and called to Izanagi. He begged her to return with him. From the shadows, Izanami told him that she would ask permission from the gods of Yomi. She warned him to stay away from her, but Izanagi was consumed with desire to see his wife again, and he lit a torch and descended into the gloom of Yomi. Finally, by the glow of his torch light, Izanagi saw that Izanami was no longer his beautiful wife, but a rotting corpse covered with maggots. Furious that her husband

Izanagi dips his jewelled spear into the ocean while Izanami watches. The droplets falling from the spear form the first island of Japan. This magnificent hanging scroll was painted by Japanese artist Kobayashi Eitaku 1843–1890).

Shinto Gods and Goddesses

The word *Shinto* means "way of the gods." In its earliest form, Shinto was not a unified religion with strict rules or beliefs. The Japanese prayed to a number of different gods and spirits, called kami. Most of the kami represented the awesome forces of nature such as the sun, the moon, the wind, and the ocean.

Izanagi and his sister and wife, Izanami, were the two gods who gave birth to the Japanese islands and several other important Japanese gods, including Amaterasu, Tsuki Yomi, and Susano.

Amaterasu, the goddess of the sun and the ruler of the High Plains of Heaven, detested her two brothers: Tsuki Yomi, the god of the moon, and Susano, the god of storms. Because of her anger, the sun and the moon sat in heaven with their backs to each other—hence day and night.

Susano was the god of storms. In many stories, he is needlessly destructive and cruel. In others, he is kind and wise. Susano was eventually banished from the High Plains of Heaven and dwelled as a god in Izumo, an area in western Japan.

Isnari, god of agriculture, rice, and prosperity, was a very important god in Japan, where the population lived off of the rice harvest. Isnari's messenger was the fox.

The Tengu are minor gods that are half human and half bird, similar to fairies in Europe. Mischievous and expert swordsmen, they live in trees in the forest.

The Oni are evil, cruel spirits that look like devils. They inflict disease, famine, and a host of other miseries on people. They can also possess innocent people and steal souls.

had ignored her warning, Izanami and the howling spirits of Yomi chased Izanagi. When Izanagi had at last reached the entrance to Yomi, he rolled a boulder across the opening, shutting in Izanami and the foul spirits and placing a permanent barrier between life and death.

How did Izanagi create three gods?

After his exhausting chase out of Yomi, Izanagi purified himself in a clear stream. He washed the filth and rot of the underworld from his face, which created more gods. He wiped his right eye and created Tsuki Yomi, god of the moon. From his left eye, he created Amaterasu, goddess of the sun. He wiped his nose and created Susano, god of storms.

Why did Amaterasu and Susano quarrel?

Izanagi assigned each of the three gods to a different realm. Tsuki Yomi controlled the night, Amaterasu, the sun goddess, ruled the High Plains of Heaven, and Susano watched over the ocean. This arrangement satisfied everyone but Susano, who pouted angrily. Amaterasu suspected that Susano would challenge her rule in heaven. Preparing for battle, she armed herself with a bow and filled two quivers with arrows. But Susano had no intention of battling Amaterasu. Instead, he proposed a contest. Whoever could create the most gods would win. To begin, ...'s sword and broke it into three pieces in her mouth and spit out responded by taking Amaterasu's ating five gods.

1057119991

ngame - Main

...ry and celebrated by ravaging the ...ughtering a pony. As a last outra-... pony's carcass into the building ...er maidens wove sacred clothing. ...t herself in a cave and refused to ...orld was covered in darkness.

...t Amaterasu out of her cave?

...ding in her cave, disaster struck the ...ntended and trees withered. Facing ...ods met together to determine how ...n the cave. They thought up a complicated plan. First, they hung a magical mirror in a tree just outside the cave entrance. Next, the young goddess of laughter, Uzume, climbed onto a bathtub and began an outrageous dance. While some gods played music, others watched the dancing and roared with laughter. The commotion shook the ground and penetrated to Amaterasu's cave. Curious, Amaterasu peeked out and asked Uzume why she was dancing. Uzume called back that they were rejoicing the appearance of another goddess far superior in beauty to Amaterasu. While Uzume spoke to Amaterasu, two gods aimed the mirror in Amaterasu's direction. She glimpsed a magnificent image in the mirror and came out of the cave to look more closely. As she gazed intently, a god slipped a magic rope across the entrance of the cave,

blocking it. Despite her realization that she was tricked, Amaterasu returned to her place in the heavens, and the sun has never failed to shine since.

What happened to Susano?

After Amaterasu returned to the High Plains of Heaven, the other gods grew impatient with Susano's mischief and banished him to earth. Bitter and angry, Susano left heaven and arrived on earth near a river. As he watched the flowing water, he noticed a pair of chopsticks drift by. Susano assumed that people were nearby, and he followed the river upstream to find them. He soon discovered an elderly couple and a young woman sitting together, weeping. He

In a brilliant burst of light, Amaterasu emerges from her cave and restores sunshine to the world. This large, colorful, highly detailed painting was created by Japanese artist Utagawa Kunisada (1785–1864).

asked them what was wrong, and the couple told Susano that a hideous, eight-headed dragon had eaten seven of their children and was now coming to take their youngest daughter. Susano revealed to them that he was a god and that he would slay the monster in exchange for the daughter's hand in marriage. After the couple happily agreed, Susano built a fence with eight openings. Behind each opening, he placed a bowl of sake—a rice wine. When the hissing dragon appeared, he plunged each of his heads into the bowls of sake and began drinking greedily. When the dragon staggered about drunk, Susano jumped from his hiding place and hacked him to death. In triumph, he married the young girl, and together they had many children.

How did the white rabbit lose its hair?

On a lonely island off the coast of Japan, a white rabbit looked longingly at the mainland. But he couldn't swim, and there was no bridge. The cunning rabbit thought of a plan to escape the island. He asked a crocodile if there were more crocodiles or rabbits on the lonely island. He persuaded the crocodile to gather his family together in a row, so the rabbit could count them. The row of crocodiles formed a bridge that would allow him to cross to the mainland. The rabbit jumped across each crocodile, counting out loud. But the rabbit could not contain his glee, and before he got to the mainland, he shouted that he was actually pulling a ruse. Enraged, the last crocodile captured him in his teeth and sheared the rabbit. Barely alive and without his fur, the miserable rabbit was left on the beach.

How did the rabbit regain his fur?

One day, a young man named Okuninushi and his eighty brothers all journeyed to a beautiful princess's palace. Each brother hoped to win her love. Since Okuninushi was the youngest, he traveled at the back of the wagon train. The band came upon the hairless rabbit, lying beside the road in great pain. Okuninushi's brothers told the suffering rabbit to bathe in salt water. But they were only tormenting the rabbit, and the poor animal's skin burned. Okuninushi had pity, and he told the rabbit to wash himself with pure water and roll in pollen from a special grass. The remedy worked, and soon the rabbit grew a gleaming coat of white fur. The rabbit explained to Okuninushi that he was actually a god, and he repaid Okuninushi's kindness by telling him that a princess would be his bride.

What were Okuninushi's ordeals?

Okuninushi's eighty brothers were furious when they heard of the white rabbit's promise. They resolved to murder Okuninushi by rolling a heated boulder down a hill onto him. Okuninushi, believing it was a wild boar, leaped out to capture it. As he seized the boulder, the rock burned through his flesh and killed him. Wailing with grief, Okuninushi's mother successfully begged the gods to restore him to life.

Finding Okuninushi still alive, the brothers tried again, this time by rigging a giant tree to fall on him as he strolled down a path. Again, the brothers were successful, and Okuninushi was left dead beneath the tree. But his mother, once again, convinced the gods to restore him to life. Fearing for her son's life, she persuaded Okuninushi to ask the god Susano for advice to end the feud.

What advice did Susano give Okuninushi?

When Okuninushi arrived in Susano's palace, he immediately fell in love with Susano's daughter, Suseri Hime. After only a few days, Okuninushi convinced her to marry him, and together they told the news to Susano. Susano was outraged at how quickly the two lovers had reached their decision. Instead of displaying his anger, however, Susano acted delighted and invited Okuninushi to sleep in a special room. But the room was full of deadly snakes, and Okuninushi only escaped because his bride had given him a magic scarf. Okuninushi waved the scarf three times, and the snakes slithered away. The next night, Okuninushi slept in a room full of centipedes. Again, the magic scarf saved his life.

Frustrated, Susano shot an arrow into a field and ordered Okuninushi to retrieve it. Once Okuninushi disappeared into the tall grass, Susano lit the field on fire. Terrified, Okuninushi watched the crackling flames creep closer. Then a mouse appeared at his foot and told him to stomp his feet. Okuninushi raised his foot and crashed it down, breaking a hole in the earth. He slipped into the

The Imperial Family

Until Japan's defeat in World War II, the Japanese emperor was worshipped as a god. The imperial family claimed its right to rule Japan because they were descended from Amaterasu, the sun goddess. The legendary first emperor of Japan was Jimmu-tenno, who conquered and united parts of Japan with the help of the gods some time in the fourth century. The imperial family has maintained an unbroken line for almost 1,500 years. In 1989, Emperor Akihito became emperor and is said to be the 125th in his line.

hole, and the fire passed harmlessly overhead. The mouse returned the arrow to Okuninushi.

By now, Okuninushi planned to flee with Suseri Hime and marry her. One evening, while Susano slumbered in his chair, Okuninushi quietly tied the god's hair to the ceiling rafters. He then stole Susano's mighty bow and sword and with Suseri Hime, mounted a horse and galloped off. The noise awoke Susano, who freed himself and chased after them. When he finally came within shouting distance, Susano decided to let the couple leave in peace. He shouted some advice to Okuninushi: the way to achieve peace with his brothers was to defeat them with the sword and bow he had stolen.

What do the Shinto Japanese believe happens to the sinful after death?

After death, evil people descend to Jigoku, a world with eight realms of fire and eight realms of ice. Each soul stands before a mirror that reflects back its sins. The god, Emma-ho, rules Jigoku and decides where each male soul is sent according to the severity of his crimes. Emma-ho's sister judges female souls. Demons, called Oni, inhabit both Jigoku and the earth. They bring disease, famine, and a host of other miseries to people on earth and torment the souls in Jigoku.

AUSTRALIA

Who are the Aborigines?

Today, the word *aborigine* usually denotes the original inhabitants of Australia. They arrived on that isolated continent by boat from southeast Asia more than 50,000 years ago. Through time, the Aborigines developed a complex and diverse culture made up of thousands of smaller groups, each with its own stories and myths. At the beginning of the 1800s, the Aborigines spoke more than 200 distinct languages.

What is The Dreamtime?

The Aborigines call the period of creation The Dreamtime. During The Dreamtime, the spirit ancestors of the Aborigines woke from their sleep and wandered through the world, creating as they traveled. They discovered bundles of animals and plants lying scattered on the ground. The ancestors carved arms, legs, and faces in the materials from the bundles to make the first human beings. The humans gathered in clans and honored the animal or plant from which they were created.

Other ancestors walked through the landscape, leaving valleys, mountains, stones, trees, or waterholes in their wake. One blind woman walked to the north, leaving a trail of water in her footsteps. The water cut the northern land into islands.

Some ancestors traveled in human form, others took the shape of kangaroos, lizards, snakes, and birds. They left markings—rocks, caves, and creeks—to indicate where they had camped or hunted during their travels. Today, aborigines consider these markings sacred spots that pulse with the creative energy of the ancestors.

How were the sun, moon, and animals created?

The world began its existence shrouded in darkness and cold. There was no life or movement—no plants, no wind, and no sounds. All spirits and gods lay slumbering. Then, Baiame, the Great Spirit, called to the goddess Yhi to come to him. Yhi shook the sleep from her body and opened her eyes, causing light to stream across the dark universe. Baiame told Yhi to descend to the earth and shine forth her light and create life.

Wherever Yhi stepped, grass, trees, and animals leapt up with life. She entered caverns that led deep into the earth and melted the ice that had collected there for so long. The landscape burst into color, sound, and life. Her job complete, Yhi transformed into the sun and took her place in the sky. When Yhi disappeared beneath the mountains in the evening, the rivers and oceans tried to follow her. With her return in the morning, they fell back to the earth as dew and mist. Yhi had pity on the animals, who were terrified of the night. Just before dawn, she set Morning Star in the heavens. But Morning Star was lonely, and so Yhi created a husband for her— the moon.

How did the animals become the way they are today?

The first animals cried out and complained to Yhi about their bodies. Kangaroo wanted stronger hind legs and a tail. Seal hated running through the forests, instead, he longed to swim in the sea. Lizard was tired of scraping his belly on the ground and wanted legs. Yhi agreed to all their requests, but warned them that the changes were probably not going to satisfy them. She was right. Owl wanted large eyes to see in the dark, but now the owl cannot enjoy the sunlight and must spend its days hiding in a tree trunk. Some mice, hoping to fly, became bats. But they did not grow beautiful feathers like birds.

This drawing of snakes was made by a contemporary Aboriginal artist, George Tjan-gala. It shows the continuing use of snake imagery.

Where did death come from?

A man named Widjingara was the first person to die. After he was killed in a fight, his wife, the Black-Headed Python, wrapped his body in bark and put him on a burial platform. She mourned the loss of her husband bitterly, and she shaved off her hair and rubbed ashes all over her

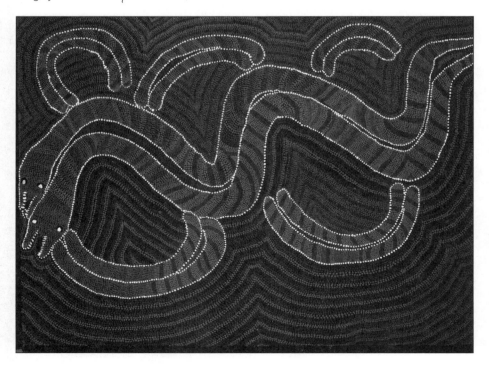

The Rainbow Serpent

The Rainbow Serpent is a powerful figure in Aboriginal mythology, and each Aboriginal tribe has its own myths about it. The Aborigines believed that the rainbow serpent dwelled in rivers, pools, and lakes. When the rainbow serpent became angry, it left its watery home and caused storms in the sky. When its anger waned, the storm ended and you can see its rainbow in the sky.

face and body to show her grief. Today, the Aborigines still mourn in this fashion.

Widjingara, however, was not dead long, because the gods had given the creatures on earth the ability to resurrect themselves. Widjingara jumped up from his grave and returned to his wife. Black-Headed Python, however, did not act happy to see him. "Look what I've done to myself!" she said, pointing to her head and her body covered with ash. Widjingara was so insulted by her hostile reception that he returned to his grave. Since then, the gift of resuscitation was lost, and all creatures must die.

How did Crow's feathers become black?

During The Dreamtime, Crow's feathers were white. One morning, Crow told his best friend Eagle to go hunting in the hills for kangaroo. Crow said that he would search along the lake for ducks. The two friends promised to share whatever they had caught with the other when they returned from the hunt.

Eagle spent all day searching for kangaroo but could not find any. Crow, in the meantime, dove into a lake and hid underwater. He took a hollow reed and poked it above the pond's surface so he could breathe. Soon, unsuspecting ducks began swimming by. Crow grabbed and pulled them under. When he had enough, he left the pond and cooked the birds over a fire. Then Crow returned to camp and told Eagle that he had had no success.

Each day, Crow told Eagle to fly to the hills in search of kangaroo and he went hunting for more ducks. Finally, Eagle grew suspicious, and one day he returned to the camp earlier than usual. As he approached, Eagle saw Crow frantically hiding the cooked duck under some leaves. As he got closer, Eagle spied grease on the fire's ashes and around Crow's mouth. Realizing that Crow had been lying to him all this time, Eagle grabbed Crow and threw him into the ashes. Whenever Crow jumped up, Eagle pounced and thrust him back until Crow's feathers were colored black, as they are to this day.

here did Norse mythology come from? ◆ What is the Norse story of creation? ◆ How were the sun, the moon, and the stars created? ◆ How were dwarves created? ◆ How were humans created? ◆ What was Yggdrasil? ◆ What was Jotunheim? ◆ What was Niflheim? ◆ What was Asgard? ◆ How were Asgard's walls built? ◆ How did the gods get their treasures? ◆ Who were the Vanir? ◆ How did Odin become the wisest of the gods? ◆ What are runes? ◆ What was Valhalla? ◆ How did Thor lose his hammer? ◆ Who was Jormungand? ◆ How did Thor come to battle the Midgard Serpent? ◆ What happened when Thor went

NORTHERN EUROPEAN CULTURES

NORSE

Where did Norse mythology come from?

Norse mythology was created in northern Europe—in the dense forests of Germany and the harsh, frozen land-scapes of Scandinavia. The Norse myths that we remember today were told mostly during the Viking era, 750–1050 A.D., when Vikings sailed their ships to loot and plunder the towns of neighboring lands.

The creators of Norse myths were an exciting people who searched for adventure and valued courage as the greatest virtue. Many Norse myths recount tales of heroes and heroines risking their lives in search of riches, adventure, and immortality. But in their icy, dark climate, the Norse also developed a tragic sense of life and inescapable destiny. Despite bravery, honor, and strength, no man or god could escape death.

What is the Norse story of creation?

In the beginning, two worlds existed, separated by an empty void called Ginnungagap. The northern world, called Niflheim, was locked in snow and ice. The southern world, Muspell, blazed with red-hot sparks and fire. From Niflheim, twelve rivers of freezing water flowed into Ginnungagap and filled it with ice. Flames from Muspell melted some of this ice into mist. The droplets formed the first creature—a giant named Ymir. As Ymir slept, a male and female frost giant grew from the sweat under his left arm and another frost giant emerged from Ymir's feet.

A giant cow called Audhumla was also born from the ice. Ymir and the frost giants lived by drinking the cow's milk. Audhumla survived by licking the salty ice that covered Niflheim. One day while she satisfied her appetite, she uncovered a man called Buri.

Buri had three grandsons—Odin, Vili, and Ve. The three brothers grew tired of Ymir, who ruled the world as a tyrant. Together, they surrounded Ymir and stabbed him to death. An ocean of blood poured from Ymir's body, drowning all of the frost giants except for two, who escaped by clinging to a hollow tree trunk.

The three brothers then created the world from Ymir's body. His blood formed the oceans, rivers, and lakes. His flesh became the earth. His bones were thrust into mountains, and his teeth became rocks and pebbles. His massive skull formed the dome of the sky, and the strands of his hair became the trees of the forest. His brains were scattered in the sky as clouds.

How were the sun, the moon, and the stars created?

To fashion the stars, the gods took blazing sparks from Muspell and set them into the sky. To give the world light and warmth, they created a girl called Sun and a boy called Moon and set them in their paths across the heavens. Both Sun and Moon had to travel quickly, because they were pursued by a pack of howling wolves. The Norse believed that the greatest of the wolves would eventually capture Sun and swallow her whole. When this happened, the world would come to an end.

How were dwarves created?

Odin, Vili, and Ve created a race of dwarves from the worms and maggots eating Ymir's body. Like worms, the dwarves live and breed below the ground's surface. The dwarves became expert craftsmen, and the gods relied upon their skill to create weapons and sparkling treasures. If the dwarves ventured into sunlight, they turned to stone, which explained the large numbers of small rocks scattered throughout Scandinavia. It is said that the dwarves can be heard whispering to each other among the mountains and canyons—we call these whisperings echoes.

How were humans created?

While walking together on a beach, Odin, Vili, and Ve discovered two logs washed in from the sea. They picked them up and from them fashioned the first man and woman, Ask and Embla. Each god gave gifts to the humans. Odin gave them life; Vili gave them understanding and the ability to move; and Ve provided speech, hearing, and sight. The three brothers placed the humans in the world they had just created from Ymir's body. They called this world Midgard.

What was Yggdrasill?

At the center of the universe stood a mighty tree, called Yggdrasill. The branches of Yggdrasill stretched into the heavens and three giant roots supported its trunk from below. Entwined within Yggdrasill's roots and branches stood nine separate worlds—each with its own race of beings. Beside one root lay Urd's well, a sacred pool of water guarded by the three Norns. The Norns watered Yggdrasill's roots and decided the fate of each man and woman. Their names were Urd (Fate), Verdandi (the Present), and Skuld (the Future). Every day, the gods gath-

(continued on page 94)

Norse gods are the source for four of our day names—Friday comes from Frigga; Thursday from Thor; Wednesday from Odin; and Tuesday from Tyr.

Yggdrasill's Many Worlds

Nine worlds existed within the tree branches and roots of Yggdrasill.

Asgard	—home to the main family of Norse gods called the Aesir
Jotunheim	—home to the frost giants
Midgard	—home to humans
Vanaheim	—home to another, less powerful, family of Norse gods called the Vanir
Alfheim	—home to a happy, kind race of elves
Nidavellir	—home to the dwarves
Svartalfheim	—home to an evil race of elves
Hel	—home to the unworthy dead
Niflheim	—the underworld

The Norse Gods

Odin ruled a race of Norse gods called the Aesir. Like the gods in Greek and Roman mythology, each god had a defining trait.

The wisest and most powerful of the Norse gods, Odin (also called Woden or Wotan) mastered the arts of magic and poetry. Odin cherished courage, and he welcomed brave warriors into his hall to feast with the gods. Two ravens flew throughout the world and returned to his shoulder at night, telling him of the events that had occurred during the day. The ravens were called Hugin and Munin—thought and memory. He carried a magical spear that never missed its target and rode an eight-legged horse, named Sleipnir, that was swifter than any horse on earth.

Frigga was Odin's wife. Like Odin, she was wise and knew of future events, although she never revealed the information to anyone.

Thor, the god of thunder, was the eldest son of Odin. He wore a belt that doubled his strength and wielded a magic hammer that always returned to his hand after striking an enemy. Brave and upright, Thor rode into battle on a bronze chariot drawn by two rams.

Balder was the son of Odin and Frigga. Handsome and fair-haired, Balder was also wise and merciful, making him most beloved of all the gods.

Tyr (also known as Tiv or Tiw) was another son of Odin and Frigga and the god who gave victory in battle. Tyr lost his right hand to the vicious wolf Fenrir.

Njord was the gentle god of the sea. He helped sailors in distress and blessed farmers with children and crops. Njord was not a member of the Aesir but of an elder race of gods called the Vanir. He was sent to Asgard, the stronghold of the Aesir, as part of a peace treaty between the warring Vanir and Aesir.

Frey, the god of the harvest and fertility, was the son of Njord. He controlled sunlight and rain, nurturing the plants of the earth and spreading peace. Frey, like his father and sister, is of the Vanir.

Freyja was Frey's twin sister and the goddess of love and beauty. She traveled through the world in a chariot drawn by two cats and was well-versed in magic and spells.

Heimdall kept watch over Bifrost Bridge, the rainbow bridge leading into Asgard. His keen hearing allowed him to hear even the sound of grass growing, and his sharp eyesight could spot objects more than one hundred miles away.

Loki, the fire god, was the son of two giants and was raised as

This Norse tapesty, woven in the 1100s, depicts three important Norse gods. Odin, missing an eye, stands on the left and carries an axe. Thor stands next to him, holding his mighty hammer. Frey, god of the harvest and fertility, stands on the right and holds an ear of corn.

Odin's foster brother. Cunning and clever, Loki could change shape at will and used his tricks to both help and hurt the other gods. Whenever there was trouble among the gods, Loki usually had a role in it.

Hel was goddess of the underworld, where men and women who died of sickness and old age spent their afterlife. One half of Hel's face was human while the other half was blank.

The highest mountain in Iceland is called Jokul, which comes from the word Jotun, meaning giant.

(continued from page 91)

ered at the well to witness and pass judgment on the deeds of men and women.

What was Jotunheim?

After escaping the flood of Ymir's blood that drowned the other giants, the giant Bergelmir and his wife sailed to a far land and gave birth to a new race of frost and mountain giants. The land—Jotunheim—existed in the mountainous and icy regions of the North, where snowstorms howled throughout the year. The giants never forgave the Aesir for the brutal murder of Ymir, and they became the deadly enemies of both people and the gods. During the long winter months, they shook their bodies, causing devastating avalanches that crushed Viking villages and swallowed the inhabitants in snow and ice. In the spring, they sent killing frosts that nipped tender tree buds and brought disease. The giants also hated sunlight because they were turned to stone whenever a sunbeam touched their flesh. Many mountains in Scandinavia were formed when careless and foolish giants did not return to shelter before dawn.

What was Niflheim?

Niflheim was a dark, frozen, fog-filled land that was home to all humans who died of disease or old age. A hideous dragon called Nidhogg survived in Niflheim by eating the flesh of human corpses. Nidhogg also gnawed at Yggdrasill's main root, hoping to bring the tree and the entire world crashing down. As a final indication of his horrible character, Nidhogg sent a mischievous squirrel scrambling up Yggdrasill's trunk to whisper insults in the ear of an eagle and a hawk perched in the top branches.

What was Asgard?

Asgard was home to the race of Norse gods called the Aesir. Surrounded by a mighty wall that protected them from enemies, each god and goddess lived in a spectacular hall. Odin dwelled in a silver-roofed hall supported by gold pillars. From his throne, he could observe all the other worlds at once. At the end of the day, the gods gathered together to feast on an endless supply of pork and a special honey ale called mead. The only entrance to Asgard was a rainbow bridge guarded by the vigilant god Heimdall. The bridge connected Asgard and Midgard. When the Norse saw a rainbow, they believed that a god had come down among them.

How were Asgard's walls built?

After the magnificent halls of Asgard were complete, a mysterious stranger offered to surround Asgard with a stone wall to protect the gods against their enemies. The man claimed to be a great stonemason, so Loki suggested that he complete the task in six months. The man agreed, and for payment he asked for the sun, the moon, and the beautiful goddess Freyja. The gods laughed among themselves, convinced that no one could complete the walls in such a short time. But the stranger had the help of a powerful stallion, who tirelessly hauled stones day and night. Stunned, the gods watched as the walls climbed higher and higher. With only three days left in the six-month period, it was obvious that the stonemason would keep his side of the deal. As the gods began to panic, Loki devised a plan to foil him. He turned himself into a lovely female horse and lured the stonemason's stallion away. Without the stallion, the stonemason was unable to finish the walls. Enraged, he began to yell and shout, and his body swelled immensely in size, revealing his true identity—a frost giant! Immediately, Thor crashed his mighty hammer onto the giant's head, toppling him to the ground, dead.

How did the gods get their treasures?

Loki's tricks could be amusing, but other times they almost led to his, or someone else's, destruction. One day, Loki cut off the shimmering golden hair of Sif, Thor's wife. When Thor saw his bald wife, he angrily caught Loki and raised his hammer threateningly. Loki pleaded for his life and promised Thor that he would restore Sif's hair. Loki then traveled to Svartalfheim, home of the dwarves, and asked them to create fantastic and wonderful things.

The masterful dwarves spun shimmering new hair out of gold for Sif. Then, they fashioned a razor-sharp spear, called Gungrir, that always struck its target. As their masterpiece, they built a mighty ship called Skidbladnir that could be folded up like cloth and stored in a pocket.

Loki then traveled to another workshop, where he described these stunning creations to two dwarves, Brokk and Eitri. Loki wagered his head that the two dwarves could not make three items to rival the ones he had just described. Brokk and Eitri agreed to the bet and eagerly went to work. First, they created a boar with golden bristles that could run over sea or land. For their second piece, they hammered a giant gold ring and decorated it with intricate carvings. Every ninth night, the ring magically created eight golden copies of itself. Loki feared that they might win the bet, so as they labored, Loki transformed himself into a fly and buzzed around their eyes, trying to distract them from their work. The two dwarves were finishing a magnificent hammer, called Mjollnir, when the fly stung one of the dwarves on the eyelid. Angrily, he raised his hand to brush it away. The finished hammer was stunning to behold, and it always shattered its target and returned to the thrower's hand. But the distraction of the fly had given the hammer one small flaw—its handle was too short.

The dwarves carried their gifts to Asgard and asked the gods to judge whether their work surpassed the hair, spear, and boat fashioned in Svartalfheim. Each god gasped at the beauty of the masterpieces. Odin took the spear and the ring, called Draupnir, for himself. Frejya was given the boar. Thor took the hammer as his own weapon.

Finally, the gods decided that the magic hammer was the greatest work, and Eitri and Brokk were declared the winners. Now, the two dwarves demanded their payment—Loki's head. Thor agreed that the gods should keep their word, and he raised his sword above Loki's neck. But Loki shouted at him to stop. He had promised his head, he explained, but he did not include any part of his neck—so Thor could not cut it. Enraged at being thwarted, the dwarves sewed Loki's lips together with leather string as punishment for his deception.

Who were the Vanir?

The Vanir were an older race of Norse gods who warred with the Aesir for control of the world. Finally, both

A 19th-century print depicts Odin as he sits on his throne and broods over the fate of humans and immortals. Two ravens, representing thought and memory, sit above him and whisper in his ears the events that occurred in the world.

sides concluded that the war was ruinous and agreed to peace. To seal the agreement, the Vanir sent three gods—Frey, Freyja, and Njord—to live with the Aesir in Asgard. To Vanaheim, the home of the Vanir, the Aesir sent Honrir, who was very handsome, and Mimir, who was Odin's uncle and known for his wisdom and knowledge.

But soon the Vanir suspected that they had been cheated. While Frey, Freyja, and Njord taught the Aesir valuable skills, Honrir appeared indecisive and foolish, especially when Mimir was absent. Enraged, the Vanir cut off Mimir's head and sent it to Asgard. Odin immediately used his magic on the head, swabbing it with herbs to ward off decay and chanting spells to give it speech. He then placed Mimir's head at the Well of Knowledge, a magic pool of water below the main root of Yggdrasill. The Well of Knowledge offered Mimir's wisdom to anyone who drank from it.

How did Odin become the wisest of the gods?

Odin loved the clash of arms in battle, but he also tirelessly sought wisdom and knowledge. While the other gods feasted and joked, Odin sat quietly on his throne, listening intently as his two ravens whispered the day's events into his ear. After the ravens left, he spent his time sipping mead and pondering what the ravens had told him. To gain more wisdom, Odin asked Mimir if he could drink from the Well of Knowledge. Mimir granted Odin's request on one condition—that he cast one of his eyes into the pool as payment. Odin agreed, trading the sight of two eyes for the greater vision provided by wisdom.

Odin wanted to know all things—past, present, and future. To gain further insight, Odin hung himself from Yggdrasill's branches for nine days and died after piercing his own body with his own spear. After he resurrected himself through magic, Odin's knowledge included the wisdom of the dead.

Who was Idun?

Idun was the goddess of spring and protector of a magical tree filled with golden apples that restored youth to whoever ate them. Every year, Idun picked the apples and carried them to Asgard, where the gods feasted on them and thus stayed young forever.

Other creatures eagerly sought the magical apples. Once, a giant named Thiazi captured Loki to get Idun's apples. In exchange for his life, Loki was forced to promise to bring Idun to Thiazi. Loki returned to Asgard and lured Idun out of the walls, where Thiazi waited in ambush. He pounced on her and returned to his lair.

Without Idun and the golden apples, the gods in Asgard began to age. Loki's role in the kidnapping was discovered, and the gods demanded that he find Idun and return her to Asgard. Loki turned himself into a falcon and flew to Thiazi's home. While Thiazi was out fishing, Loki found Idun and turned her into a nut. Clasping the nut in his claws, Loki flew back to Asgard. Thiazi soon discovered Idun's absence and flew to Asgard as an eagle. But the gods were waiting for him. After Loki landed in Asgard, the gods lit huge bonfires along the walls. The leaping flames singed Thiazi's wings, and he crashed to the earth, where the gods stabbed him to death.

What was Valhalla?

Valhalla was an enormous hall that housed the Einherjar, warriors who had died heroically in battle. More than five hundred doors opened into the hall, allowing more than eight hundred warriors to march through each door at once. Odin himself sat at the head of the hall with his two wolves and trusty ravens, sipping wine as the warriors enjoyed an endless feast of boar meat and mead. To keep fit, the warriors strapped on their armor and fought each other every day. All warriors who were slain or wounded during that day's battle were resurrected that evening before the meal. Odin planned to use the warriors as his army in the final battle between good and evil.

How did Thor retrieve his lost hammer?

One day, Thor was shocked to discover that his hammer was missing. Desperate, he asked Loki to find it. Loki turned himself into a falcon and soared above the earth, searching for clues to the hammer's disappearance. Finally, Loki learned that a frost giant named Thrym had stolen the hammer and hidden it deep beneath a mountain in the icy land of Jotunheim. When Loki tried to retrieve the hammer, he found out that Thrym would not return the hammer unless he was given the beautiful goddess Freyja to be his wife.

As Freyja screamed in rage at this proposal, the god Heimdall came up with a plan. He proposed that Thor disguise himself as Freyja in a bride's dress and journey to Thrym's home. Loki would also go along, dressed as a bridesmaid. At first, Thor protested against the embarrassment of wearing a dress, but Loki reminded him that he was powerless without his hammer.

Reluctantly, Thor put on the wedding dress, covered his face with a veil, and arrived at Thrym's hall. At the wedding feast, Thrym was stunned as his new bride displayed an incredible appetite, easily eating an ox and eight salmon. Loki explained that the bride was so excited by the wedding that she had fasted for eight days. When Thrym tried to kiss his bride, Thor's eyes glowed behind the veil, and he drew back in terror. Again, Loki explained that the bride was so eager for her new husband, that she had not slept for eight nights.

At last, Thor's hammer was brought into the hall to bless the new couple. As Thrym looked on in shock, Thor tore off his dress and seized the hammer in fury. Within moments, every giant in the hall lay dead, and Loki and Thor returned to Asgard in triumph.

Who was Jormungand?

Loki had three monstrous children—the wolf Fenrir, the fearful goddess Hel, and Jormungand, a giant serpent. When Odin saw the serpent, he was filled with fear and disgust, and he cast the serpent from Asgard into the ocean. There it grew so large that it encircled the entire world and became known as the Midgard Serpent. Sailors who ventured far from land feared that the serpent would emerge from the ocean's depths and destroy them with its jaws and venom.

How did Thor come to battle the Midgard Serpent?

Thor, who often sought out challenges to his strength, decided to slay the Midgard Serpent. According to one story, Thor disguised himself as a young boy and journeyed to the oceanside home of a giant called Hymir. Thor asked if he could join the giant on his next fishing trip. Hymir did not like the idea but allowed Thor to accompany him. Thor chopped off the head of one of Hymir's oxen for bait and returned to the boat. The two set out, and Thor rowed so quickly that soon they were far beyond the sight of land. Sensing that the serpent was near, Thor placed the ox head on the hook and cast it over board. They waited. Suddenly, the ocean churned as the Midgard Serpent seized the bait in its jaws. Thor grabbed the line and began hauling the serpent toward the boat. But the boat couldn't support Thor and his feet crashed through the floor and hit

Thor raises his mighty hammer in this striking black-and-white drawing by noted 19th-century illustrator Arthur Rackham.

the bottom of the ocean. Now that he stood on firm ground, Thor began dragging the hissing serpent closer and closer. He raised his hammer and was about to crush the serpent's skull, when Hymir panicked and cut the line. As the serpent slithered away to safety, Thor roared with anger and threw Hymir overboard. Thor and the Midgard Serpent are destined to battle again at Ragnarok, the doom of the Norse gods.

What happened when Thor went to Utgard?

In the icy land of Jotunheim, the frost giants built a fortress called Utgard. Thor decided to journey to Utgard and do battle with the giants who lived there. To help him, Thor brought Loki and two human servants called Thialfi and Roskva. While traveling to Utgard, Thor and his three companions sought shelter for one night in a massive hall with several giant doorways. Thor marveled at its size. In the morning, they discovered that the hall was actually a glove for the giant Skrymir, who lay sleeping nearby. Enraged by the giant's snores, Thor slammed his hammer down on Skrymir's forehead. But the giant merely shrugged off the blows and wondered if a leaf had fallen upon him. Thor continued on and arrived at Utgard. Again, Thor was amazed at the size of the hall and the frost giants who lived there, but he was still determined to beat them at contests of strength and skill. Unfortunately, Thor, Loki, and Thialfi did not perform as well as they expected. Loki lost an eating contest; Thialfi was defeated in a foot race; and Thor lost both a drinking contest and a wrestling match with an old woman.

Shocked and dismayed, Thor admitted that they were beaten. As Thor and his companions left Utgard, a giant explained that the frost giants had used magic and illusion to defeat them. Loki had actually competed with fire, which quickly and ceaselessly devours things in its flames. Thialfi had raced against the speed of his own thought. In the drinking contest, Thor had drunk from a horn that contained the ocean. Although he failed to empty the horn of its contents, Thor did succeed in lowering the sea level considerably. In the wrestling contest, Thor had actually battled old age, which is invincible. As Thor fumed at the thought of being tricked, Loki chuckled to himself, relishing the fact that clever thinking will always defeat strength.

The Norse used the story of Thor drinking the ocean to explain the rising and falling of the ocean every day, which we know as the tide.

How did Thor defeat Geirrod?

The giant Geirrod was Thor's fiercest enemy. One day, Geirrod captured Loki. In exchange for his life, the god promised to bring Thor to Gerriod's hall—without his mighty hammer. Gerriod was thrilled with the idea of defeating Thor at last.

Loki convinced Thor to go to Gerriod's hall without his hammer. Along the way, Thor and Loki stayed with a friendly giantess. She warned Thor of the trap and lent him her magic belt of strength, a magic staff, and a pair of magic gloves. When Thor and Loki arrived at Gerriod's hall, Thor was taken to a room with a single chair. He sat down on it and fell asleep. Suddenly, he felt the chair rising rapidly toward the ceiling. With his magic staff, he pressed the chair back down and heard a scream followed by a loud snap. Gerriod's two daughters lay dead beneath the chair. They had planned to crush Thor against the ceiling.

Gerriod now entered the hall. Using a pair of tongs, he picked a red-hot iron ball from the fire and flung it at Thor. Thor caught the ball with his magic gloves and aimed it back at him. The iron ball crashed through an iron column and slammed into Gerriod's body, killing him.

Who was Andvari?

Andvari was a craftsman dwarf whose treasure was seized by Loki. Once, while traveling through Midgard with Odin and Honir, Loki killed an otter for dinner. They traveled on to a farmhouse and offered to share the otter with the farmer Hreidmar. In horror, Hreidmar told them that the otter was his son. Hreidmar and his two other sons weakened the gods with magic, rendering them helpless to their attack. In reparation for the otter's death, Loki offered to give Hreidmar enough gold to cover the otter's skin. The skin, however, was magical and could be stretched to an immense size. So, while Odin and Honir stayed at the farm as hostages, Loki searched for a giant treasure.

Loki borrowed a magic net from a sea goddess and descended through a maze of tunnels to an underground lake. There, he captured a large pike that was actually the dwarf Andvari. Loki was in luck. Andvari owned a massive and beautiful treasure. To secure his freedom, Andvari bitterly agreed to surrender his wealth to Loki. Watching in fury as Loki walked off with his hoard of gold, Andvari laid a terrible curse on a magical gold-making ring that lay within the treasure. Whoever possessed the ring would be doomed.

Who was Fafnir?

Fafnir was one of Hreidmar's sons. When he saw Andvari's fabulous treasure, he fell under the curse of the ring and plotted to murder his father for it. Helped by his brother, Regin, Fafnir carried out his deed. The greed and evil of the murder transformed Fafnir from a man into a hideous dragon. Fafnir took the treasure to a lair in the forest, where he defended it against the many warriors who tried to seize it from him.

Who was Sigurd?

Sigurd was the greatest hero of Norse mythology. Like many other ambitious men, Sigurd hoped to slay Fafnir and take his treasure. Accompanied by Fafnir's brother, Regin, Sigurd searched for the dragon. Finally, they found the tracks it made as it traveled from its lair to drink at a river. Regin suggested to Sigurd that he dig a trench along the path and lie down in it. When the dragon passed by, Sigurd stabbed his sword into its soft underbelly, slicing it open and killing it. Afterwards, Regin asked Sigurd to cut open the dragon and give him the heart. Later, Sigurd roasted the heart over a fire while Regin drifted off to sleep. To test the meat, Sigurd ran his fingers over the heart and licked the blood. Suddenly, he could understand the birds singing in the tree above him. They told him that the heart had magical powers, and that Regin wanted the treasure for himself. Enraged, Sigurd sliced off Regin's head and ate the dragon's heart. The birds then told Sigurd to find a Valkyrie named Brynhild. She would give him more knowledge and wisdom.

Who was Brynhild?

Brynhild was a Valkyrie who disobeyed Odin's orders. As punishment, he condemned her to endless sleep in a bed surrounded by a ring of fire. Only the bravest warrior could pass through the ring and wake her. Sigurd saw the blazing ring from a distant hill and rode his horse unharmed through the flames. The spell was broken, and

The Valkyries

The Valkyries were female demi-goddesses who roamed over bloody battlefields in search of brave warriors. (A demigod or demigoddess was stronger than a mortal but not as powerful as god.) When they found a truly brave warrior, the Valkyries would take them to Odin, who welcomed him into paradise at Valhalla. The Norse believed that the bravest fighters saw the Valkyries just before dying in combat.

Brynhild gazed with delight at Sigurd, who had already fallen in love with Brynhild's beauty. He slipped Andvari's cursed ring onto her finger as a sign of his love and left a few days later, promising to return to her.

Sigurd then entered the service of a king. The queen saw the handsome, brave Sigurd and wanted him to marry her daughter, Gudrun. She gave him a magical potion that made him forget Brynhild, and soon he and Gudrun were married. Sigurd also became great friends with Gudrun's brother, Gunnar. Later, Gunnar told Sigurd that he had fallen in love with a woman—Brynhild! Gunnar could not cross through the ring of flame surrounding her, and he asked

This carved wood detail from the portal of a 1100s Norwegian church at Hylestad, Setesdal, shows the story of Sigurd slaying the dragon Fafnir. The portal was made of many carved wooden panels.

The Berserkers

The Berserkers were warriors inspired to madness by Odin's sorcery. They charged into battle without armor, heedless of pain or danger. Given extraordinary strength by their madness, they savagely attacked their opponents in the frenzy of combat. We still use the expression "They went berserk" to describe people who lose control in rage and anger.

The Norse legends of Brynhild and Sigurd, as well as many related tales, are recounted in the four-opera-long work by the German composer Richard Wagner called The Ring of the Nibelung *or* The Ring Cycle.

Sigurd to disguise himself as Gunnar and woo Brynhild in his place. Sigurd agreed and rode his horse through the flames once more. Brynhild, who had given up hope that Sigurd would return, left the ring of flame with "Gunnar" and became his wife.

Brynhild and Gudrun quarreled viciously over whose husband was greater. Brynhild argued that her husband was braver because he had ridden through fire to reach her. At that moment, Gudrun revealed the truth, that Gunnar had actually been Sigurd in disguise.

Brynhild plotted revenge and convinced Gunnar to have Sigurd murdered. But when Sigurd was dead, Brynhild learned that Sigurd had only forgotten her because of the magic potion. In mournful agony, she stabbed herself at Sigurd's funeral pyre and was laid at his side, thus ending the most tragic of Norse love stories.

How did Balder die?

One night, Balder's sleep was disturbed by horrible dreams that predicted his death. The next morning, the other gods heard about Balder's dreams and feared for his safety. To protect Balder, Frigga traveled through the world and demanded that everything vow never to harm Balder. Soon, all things—stones and trees, metal and animals—took the oath.

Reassured that Balder could not be harmed, the gods began tossing spears and rocks at him as a joke. The rocks fell to the ground, and the spears sailed off their mark, never harming Balder. But Loki hated Balder, and he plotted his death. By disguising himself as a woman, Loki learned from Frigga that one thing had not sworn the

This Arthur Rackham illustration shows the Valkyrie Brynhild.

oath—mistletoe. Frigga believed that the mistletoe bush was too harmless to hurt Balder.

With great cunning, Loki pulled up a mistletoe branch and convinced Hoder, a blind god, to throw it at Balder. As Loki guided his hand, Hoder hurled the mistletoe at Balder, piercing his chest and killing him.

How did the gods try to bring Balder back to life?

Balder's death plunged all of Asgard into grief. Halder, Odin's son, agreed to ride down to Hel and bring Balder back to life. Riding Sleipnir, Odin's eight-legged horse, Halder galloped swiftly down the dark road that led to the walls of Hel. Urged by Halder, Sleipner leaped over the walls and into the main hall of Hel. There he found Balder sitting on a throne with Hel sitting beside him. Hel agreed to release Balder on one condition—all things in the world had to weep for his death. If one creature resisted, then Balder would remain in Hel.

The gods sent the message throughout the world, and all things responded. Animals and men wept. Stones, metal, and trees shed tears. Finally, a messenger of the gods discovered a female giant lying alone in a cave. The giantess was none other than Loki in disguise. The messenger asked her if she mourned for Balder. Twisted by his hatred, Loki responded no. Hel heard the answer, and Balder remained in Hel.

What happened to Loki?

The gods realized that their toleration of Loki had allowed evil to grow in Asgard. They resolved to hunt him down and capture him. Loki knew that the gods would punish him severely, so when they approached, Loki changed himself into a salmon and jumped into a stream.

A wise god named Kvasir fashioned a net that finally snared Loki. As punishment for his evil, the gods fastened Loki to three stones with ropes made from the intestines of his own son. Over his head, a poisonous snake dripped venom onto his face. To ease his pain, Loki's wife, Sigun, joined him at his side and held a cup that caught the snake's venom. But every time she emptied the cup, a few drops splattered onto Loki's face. When Loki screamed in agony, the Norse believed that the entire earth shook with earthquakes.

What is Ragnarok?

Ragnarok is the time of destruction for the world and the gods. Odin, who could see the future, knew that Ragnarok would come and that resistance was useless. However, Odin and the gods planned to battle to the end. This story reflects the Norse belief that despite death, a man could win honor by fighting bravely until death.

At the beginning of Ragnarok, the world will be wracked by terrible wars, in which all honor and decency

Loki writhes in agony as his wife, Sigun, desperately tries to keep the snake's venom from dripping onto his face. When Sigun emptied the cup, the venom seared Loki's face, making him shake with pain, causing earthquakes. This scene was depicted by an anonymous 19th-century illustrator.

is corrupted by bloody atrocities. A giant wolf will swallow the sun, condemning everything to icy cold and darkness. The stars will fall from the sky, and the mountains will tumble as Yggdrasill shakes to its very roots. Hideous monsters will escape from their prisons, including the wolf Fenrir and Loki. Loki will then lead the frost giants and monsters onto the Plain of Vigrid—the site of the final battle of the gods.

Heimdall, vigilantly watching from the rainbow bridge, will blow his horn in a mighty blast, alerting all the gods that the final battle is near. From Valhalla, thousands of warriors will join the gods as they battle the giants. Thor is destined to die from the poison of the Midgard Serpent. Odin will be ripped apart by Fenrir, who will be clubbed to death by Odin's son. Loki will die fighting Heimdall. All the gods and giants will be destroyed in the battle. Finally, a fire giant named Surt will rise and fling fire in all directions, causing all nine worlds to be consumed in flames. When all things are reduced to ashes, the world will be swallowed by the sea.

Is the world restored?

Just before she is swallowed, the sun will give birth to a daughter, who will light the sky as a new sun. Under her warmth, a new world is destined to flourish. One man and one woman will escape the disaster, and together will repopulate the earth. The children of the gods will survive and restore order, beginning a new golden age of peace and prosperity.

CELTS

Who were the Celts?

The Celts were powerful warriors who sacked even the mighty city of Rome around 387 B.C.

From approximately 1000 A.D. to 100 B.C., the Celts (pronounced "Kelts") were a band of tribes that dominated northwestern Europe—northern Spain, France, Great Britain, and Ireland. We call these tribes Celts because they spoke languages that stemmed from Celtic. However, these tribes only loosely shared a common culture, and they each developed their own myths.

How do we know the Celtic myths?

From 100 B.C.. to A.D. 100, many of the Celtic tribes in Europe were conquered by Roman armies and became a part of the Roman Empire. Most of their myths are lost. However, other parts of the Celtic world—Ireland, Scotland, and parts of England—escaped Roman control. Their stories survived because Christian monks wrote down Celtic myths and legends when they arrived in Ireland and Great Britain around A.D. 500.

Who were the Firbolg?

The Firbolg were a legendary race of people who lived in Ireland. Originally, they labored as slaves in a land near Greece. They hauled bags of earth over their shoulders to cover rocky areas and make it suitable for farming (hence their name, which means "bag men"). After years of abuse, they escaped by turning their bags into boats and sailing to Ireland.

Who were the Tuatha Dé Danann?

The Tuatha Dé Danann were a race of Irish Celtic gods who arrived in Ireland after the Firbolg had already settled there. After a fierce battle, called the First Battle of Magh Tuireadh, the Tuatha Dé Danann defeated the Firbolg and drove them off the island. The Firbolg settled in the Aran Islands off the western coast of Ireland, where they built the fort of Dun Aonghusa, which can still be seen today.

The Tuatha Dé Danann brought four magical items to Ireland—the Stone of Fal, which screamed when a rightful king of Ireland sat on it; the sword of Nuada, which always struck a fatal blow; the spear of Lugh, which guaranteed victory; and the Cauldron of Dagda, which provided an endless amount of food.

Who were the Fomorians?

After driving out the Firbolg, the Tuatha Dé Danann faced a new enemy—the Fomorians. The Fomorians were an evil race of giants that lived both on Ireland and in the sea around it. The Fomorians were led by Balor, who had only one eyeball. His gaze was so deadly, he only opened his eye on the battlefield. It took four men to lift his eyelid so Balor could murder his enemies.

Who was Ethlinn?

Ethlinn was Balor's daughter. It was prophesied that Ethlinn's son would grow up to kill Balor. To prevent this, Balor locked Ethlinn in a crystal tower on a remote island off Ireland's northern coast. But a god from the Tuatha Dé Danann managed to sneak into the princess's chamber, and she later bore triplets—three sons. Balor was enraged when he discovered the birth, and he ordered that the three boys be drowned in a whirlpool. When Balor's servants wrapped the three boys into a sheet, one son fell

The term Banshee *comes from the Celtic Bean-Sidhe, meaning fairy woman. The Celts believed that whenever a banshee wailed, it foretold a person's death.*

The Irish Celtic Gods

The Irish Celts had many different gods and goddesses. Here are some of the most prominent.

Dagda, which means "the good god," was father of the Tuatha Dé Danann. Dagda carried a magical club so large that he hauled it behind him on two wheels. If he struck anything with one side of his club, it fell dead while a tap from the other side restored life. Daghda also owned an enormous cauldron that provided an endless supply of food. Many Celts worshipped him as the god of fertility.

Dian Cecht was the god of healing. He immersed dead members of Tuatha Dé Danann into a magical well and chanted spells that restored them to life. When Nuada lost his hand in battle, he fashioned a silver hand as its temporary replacement.

Nuada was a fierce warrior and leader of the Tuatha Dé Danann. Nuada's hand was cut off during the First Battle of Magh Tuireadh—earning him the name "Nuada of the Silver Hand."

Morrigan was the war goddess who flew over battlefields as a crow. Above the chaotic and bloody fighting, she decided who would live and who would die.

Goibhniu was the god of crafts. He forged deadly weapons that always struck their target. He also brewed an ale that gave the drinker immortality.

Manannan MacLir ruled the sea and practiced magic. He rode over the ocean's waves in a self-propelled boat called the Wave Sweeper.

Lugh was the handsome god of light. His bravery in battle won many victories for the Tuatha Dé Danann.

out and was saved. The boy, called Lugh, grew into a strong and handsome warrior who joined the Tuatha Dé Danann as the god of light. When the Tuatha Dé Danann faced the Fomorians in battle, Lugh saw Balor's eyelid being lifted. At that moment, Lugh raised his slingshot and fired a rock, smashing the eyeball back into Balor's skull. Now the eye faced the other direction, exposing the Fomorian army to its fierce gaze. The Fomorians panicked and scattered before the advancing Tuatha Dé Danann. This victory was called the Second Battle of Magh Tuireadh.

Who was Ith?

Ith was a man who lived in a giant tower in Spain. From the top of the tower, he could glimpse the distant shores of

Ireland. Curious about the strange land, he assembled ninety followers and set sail for the island. He arrived just after the Tuatha Dé Danann had defeated the Fomorians. Believing that Ith led yet another invasion, the Tuatha Dé Danann killed him. When Ith's family heard about his death, they vowed revenge. Ith's father, Milesius, organized an invasion force that set sail for Ireland. Although Milesius did not survive the voyage, his sons landed and struck the Tuatha Dé Danann at their stronghold at Tara. The Tuatha Dé Danann were defeated in battle and were banished to the remote hills and caves of Ireland. Milesius's descendants became the Celts and the Tuatha Dé Danann were later known as fairies, or fair folk.

Who were the Fianna?

The Fianna were a hardy band of warriors who swore to protect the king of Ireland. To join the Fianna, a man stood in a hole up to his waist, armed only with his shield and a stick. Nine warriors circled around him and threw spears. If the man warded off the deadly shafts, he became a member of the Fianna.

How did Finn MacCool grow wise?

Finn MacCool was the greatest leader of the Fianna. As a young boy, Finn was taught by the druid Finegas. One day, Finegas caught the Salmon of Knowledge. Whoever ate the magical salmon would receive incredible knowledge and wisdom. Delighted with his catch, Finegas gave the salmon

The Fianna were also called the Fenians. In 1858, Irish and Irish Americans formed a political group called the Fenians. They plotted to achieve Irish independence from Great Britain.

Druids

Druids were the political and spiritual leaders in Celtic society in what is now Britain, Ireland, and parts of France. As priests and teachers, they conducted the religious ceremonies of the Celtic tribes and studied magic. They revered the oak tree and mistletoe and often held their ceremonies in oak forests. As leaders, they exercised great power over decisions made by the tribe. Druids were assisted by female sorcerers or prophets, although only a man could be a Druid. The religion of Druidism died out after Christianity spread through northwestern Europe in the fifth and sixth centuries.

to Finn and ordered him to cook it. Finn let the fish sit over
the fire for several minutes. To see if it was done, Finn ran his
thumb over the skin. The heat burned his thumb, and he
stuck it into his mouth to cool it off. Suddenly, the fish's
knowledge and wisdom passed into Finn. From then on,
Finn could answer any question by simply placing his thumb
in his mouth. The answer would instantly appear in his head.
He called this gift "the tooth of knowledge."

Who was Diarmuid Ua Diubhne?

Diarmuid was a handsome warrior who fought with
the Fianna. After spending a day hunting in woods,
Diarmuid and three companions found shelter in a hut. A
beautiful woman owned the hut and received them warmly. However, of the four men, she chose Diarmuid to share
her bed. While the other warriors slept, she told Diarmuid
that she was the goddess of youth. She raised her finger
and lightly touched his forehead. From then on, she told
him, any woman who glimpsed that spot would instantly
fall in love with him.

Who was Grainne?

After being touched by the goddess of youth, Diarmuid
spent much of his time resisting the advances of women.
He avoided all of them except one—the beautiful Grainne,
daughter of the king of the Fianna. Unfortunately for
Diarmuid, Grainne was already engaged to Finn—the warrior leader of the Fianna. Grainne used her magic to escape
from Finn with Diarmuid. For the next sixteen years, the
two lovers were pursued relentlessly by Finn and his warriors. Finally, the king intervened, and Finn grudgingly
called off the pursuit. But Finn never forgave Diarmuid.

Years later, Diarmuid was seriously wounded while
hunting a boar, and only a magical drink of water from
Finn could save him. Finn recognized Diarmuid as he
approached him with the water cupped in his hands. Still
angry and bitter after all those years, he let the water trick-
le through his fingers, ensuring Diarmuid's death.

Who was Oisin?

Oisin was one of the sons of Finn MacCool. While on a
hunt with his companions, Finn and his dogs chased a deer

through the woods, excited at the chance for a fresh meal. But when the deer finally collapsed in exhaustion, the dogs did not attack her. Instead, they playfully licked her head and hooves. Finn was stunned by this, and he ordered no one else to harm the deer. When the hunters returned to their home, the deer followed.

That night, Finn awoke to see a beautiful woman standing next to his bed. Her name was Sadb, and she explained to him that she was under an evil spell. The spell could only be broken if Finn fell in love with her. Struck by her beauty, Finn passionately loved her and broke the spell. Weeks later, Finn returned from battle to discover that Sadb had been lured away and captured by a magician who had disguised himself as Finn. In frantic despair, Finn searched every patch of woods, every hill, and every cave in Ireland—but without success. Mournfully, he returned to his hunting life and tried to forget Sadb.

Years later, Finn came across a young boy in the woods. When Finn asked where he had come from, the boy told how a sorcerer had forced his mother to abandon him. When the boy described his mother, Finn rushed over and embraced him, for the mother was clearly Sadb, and the boy was his own son. Finn called the boy Oisin (Little Faun), and he trained him as a warrior to join the Fianna. Later, Oisin became known throughout Ireland for his beautiful poetry and songs.

How did Oisin meet St. Patrick?

As Oisin hunted along a beach, he met a goddess mounted on a horse with silver hooves and a golden mane. Her name was Niamh, daughter of the sea god Manannan. Niamh invited Oisin to join her in the ageless golden realm of the gods. Oisin accepted, mounted her horse, and together they rode off.

But after many years, Oisin yearned for his old life. Observing his depressed mood, Niamh gave him a magic horse to travel back to Ireland. Just before Oisin left, she warned him not to touch the ground, otherwise he could never return to her. Oisin returned to find a world centuries older than the one he had left. The people appeared sad-

The Celtic hero Cuchulainn is portrayed in this 1913 drawing by artist John Duncan.

der and weary. The gods were different. He came upon a wretched group of men trying to move a heavy boulder. Still mounted on his horse, Oisin reached down and easily lifted it for them. But the movement loosened his saddle, and he toppled to the ground. The moment his skin touched the earth, he was transformed from a young warrior to a crippled old man. In grief and disbelief, Oisin wandered through the countryside, asking for Finn MacCool. But no one had heard of him. The people considered Oisin mad, and they took him before St. Patrick, who listened to Oisin and wrote down his tale. Gently, St. Patrick explained to Oisin that Christ was now the god of Ireland.

Who was Cuchulainn?

Cuchulainn is Ireland's greatest Celtic hero. When he was born, it was prophesied that he would live a glorious but short life. His father was Lugh, the god of light. As a young boy, Cuchulainn demonstrated his power and strength by killing an enormous hound with his bare hands, thus earning him his name—the Hound of Culan.

Later, Cuchulainn roared into combat for the first time and experienced a horrible transformation. One eye disappeared into his skull; the other eye bulged and turned a grotesque red color. His jaw swelled until he could easily fit a man's head into his mouth. A halo, blood-red in color, surrounded his head. He howled so loudly that spirits living underground and in the hills joined him. After slaughtering many enemies in ferocious battle, it took three vats of cold water to cool him down and return him to normal.

How did Cuchulainn win his bride?

Cuchulainn fell in love with a woman named Emer. But her father, Forgall, objected to the match, claiming that Cuchulainn had not yet proven himself as a warrior. Forgall suggested that Cuchulainn make the difficult journey to the Land of Shadows to study combat with Scathach, a warrior-princess. Cuchulainn left immediately. With Scathach, Cuchulainn underwent dangerous and exhausting training. He learned the techniques of sword fighting and how to wield Scathach's magical spear. Once the spear entered the body, it expanded into thirty barbs, ensuring death.

Now a formidable warrior, Cuchulainn jumped into his chariot and galloped out of the Land of Shadows to claim Emer as his bride. Shocked at Cuchulainn's arrival, Emer's father barred the doors. Furious, Cuchulainn slaughtered Forgall's warriors and seized Emer. In the final battle, Cuchulainn chased Forgall to his castle walls, where Forgall slipped and fell to his death.

Women Warriors

A strong tradition of women warriors existed in Celtic society, where women bore arms into battle as late as A.D. 700. Reflecting this reality, many of the fiercest Celtic gods were female. One Irish war goddess was named Macha. When Macha was on the verge of giving birth, her husband told the king of Ulster that she, even while pregnant, could outrun his horses. The king of Ulster challenged this boast, and he threatened to execute Macha's husband unless she raced. In fury, Macha cursed Ulster's soldiers for five days and five nights with the pain of childbirth. Then she challenged Ulster's horses to a race and defeated them.

This image on the Gundestrup Cauldron, a silver cauldron created in the 1st century B.C., depicts a Celtic goddess with birds and children.

How did Cuchulainn kill his own son?

While Cuchulainn studied with Scathach in the Land of Shadows, he seduced her sister, Aoife. When Cuchulainn left Aoife, he gave her a gold ring, unaware that she was also pregnant with his son. Aoife named her son Conlai, and she raised him alone, teaching him to expertly wield the sword and spear. Years later, Conlai took his father's gold ring and went to Ulster, where Cuchulainn lived. Like his father, Conlai was a proud fighter and he challenged the Ulster warriors to combat. During one fight, Conlai killed Conall, Cuchulainn's foster brother. Cuchulainn swore revenge for the death and attacked the stranger. As he struck and absorbed sword thrusts, Cuchulainn admired the young man's skillful use of his weapon. But then Conlai swiped and cut a lock of Cuchulainn's hair. Cuchulainn exploded in rage and drove his magical spear into Conlai's stomach. As Conlai fell to the ground, Cuchulainn suddenly recognized the ring he had given to Aoife so many years before. Crushed with grief and guilt, Cuchulainn carried his dying son back to his home, where he bitterly mourned his loss.

Who was Queen Maeve?

Queen Maeve was the powerful warrior ruler of Connacht, a kingdom in Ireland. One night, she and her husband, Ailill, argued over who had finer possessions. They matched each other evenly except for one item— Ailill's magnificent white-horned bull. Enraged at losing the argument, Maeve searched for an animal that would match Ailill's. She learned of the Brown Bull of the kingdom of Ulster—a bull so large that fifty boys could ride on its back. Determined to own the bull, Maeve commanded her army to invade Ulster and bring it back to Connacht.

Maeve's timing was perfect. The soldiers of Ulster were paralyzed for five days and five nights by Macha's curse. Only the Ulster warrior Cuchulainn was strong enough to fight on. He met the armies of Connacht as they crossed a river into Ulster. Single-handedly, he slaughtered hundreds of Connacht soldiers and slowed their advance to a crawl. For five days, he fought alone, until finally the curse began to wear off and the Ulster soldiers formed ranks for battle. But it was too late for Cuchulainn. Exhausted and surrounded, Cuchulainn suffered a severe spear wound in his stomach. With his last breaths, he bound himself to a stone pillar so that he would die on his feet. The war goddess Morrigan, who had been spurned by Cuchulainn earlier, turned into a crow and landed on his shoulder in triumph.

Who won the contest between the Brown Bull of Ulster and the White-Horned Bull?

With Cuchulainn dead, Maeve's army seized the Brown Bull and sent it back to Connacht. When the White-Horned Bull saw the Brown Bull entering his territory, he charged. The two bulls slammed together and locked horns. For hours, their immense bodies twisted, strained, and lurched all over the island of Ireland. As the next morning's mists cleared, the Brown Bull proudly trotted back to Ulster with the White-Horned Bull dead on its horns. But before the Ulster soldiers could shout in triumph, the Brown Bull's heart burst and he collapsed, dead. Realizing the futility of more war, Connacht and Ulster agreed to peace.

How did Queen Maeve die?

A young man named Forbai, who the son of an Ulster king, was not satisfied with the peace. He swore he would get revenge for Queen Maeve's ruinous war. Forbai knew that Queen Maeve bathed every day in a pool outside her castle. One day, he slipped into Connacht and measured the exact distance between the pool where she bathed and the place where he had come ashore. He returned to Ulster and practiced firing his sling shot over that distance. When he had complete faith in his aim, Forbai traveled back to Connacht and waited tensely as Queen Maeve stepped into her pool. He loaded a rock into his sling shot and launched it, striking the queen in the forehead and killing her instantly. The invasion of Ulster was avenged.

Who were the children of Lir?

Lir, a king of the Tuatha Dé Dannann, married a woman named Aoife after his first wife died. (While Aoife has the same name as the mother of Cuchulainn's son, she is not the same woman). Aoife, the sister of Lir's first wife, pledged herself to loving and raising Lir's four children: Fionnuala, Aodh, and twin boys Fiachra and Conn. But, she grew jealous of the time and attention that her husband gave to the children. One day, Aoife suffered a fit of rage and ordered her servants to slay the four children where they stood. When the servants refused, Aoife used magic to transform Fionnuala and the three boys into four beautiful swans. Aoife told the four children that they would have to remain in the shape of swans for nine hundred years. The children would spend the first three hundred years on Lough Dairbhreach (the Lake of the Oaks), the next three hundred years on the Struthna Moyle (the Irish Sea), and the last three hundred years beside the island called Inis Gluaire. They would have to remain in the shape of swans until a woman of southern Ireland married a man of the North.

The children kept their voices and sang mournful songs of their imprisonment, which became famous throughout Ireland. After nine hundred years, the children found themselves in the South on Inis Gluaire, where the local queen, Deoch, heard them sing. Queen Deoch was a boastful and vain woman, and she wanted the swans for her own entertainment at the court. She sent her husband to capture them. Her husband, Lairgnean, was king of Connacht, in the North of Ireland. Just as Lairgnean grabbed the swans, the curse was lifted, and the children became human again. They transformed into three withered men and an ancient woman. In an instant, they turned to dust, finally free in death.

Who were Tristan and Iseult?

Tristan and Iseult were two lovers whose tale ends in tragedy. Tristan went to Ireland to woo the beautiful Iseult on behalf of his friend and king, Mark of Cornwall. Tristan approached Iseult's father, and he gave his blessing to the marriage. But Iseult was not enthusiastic about marrying King Mark. To help her daughter, Iseult's mother concocted a special love potion. She instructed Iseult's maid to give Iseult the potion on her wedding night. After drinking the potion, Iseult would fall passionately in love with King Mark and enjoy happiness for the rest of her life. While on the voyage to Cornwall, however, Tristan and Iseult accidentally drank some of the potion. They glimpsed at each other and fell madly in love.

Iseult still married King Mark, but she and Tristan met secretly. One day, King Mark discovered Tristan and Iseult asleep with Tristan's sword between them. Instead of killing them, King Mark felt pity and exchanged his sword for Tristan's. When Tristan awoke and saw the sword, he knew instantly that King Mark was aware of his affair with Iseult. Overcome with guilt, Tristan left Cornwall and settled in France. He married another woman but remained unhappy.

Tristan fought several battles while in France. During one fight, he suffered a greivous wound. Desperate, he sent for Iseult, who had cured a similar wound long before. In a letter, Tristan instructed Iseult to hoist a white sail to

Tristan accompanies Iseult (wearing a crown) on their ill-fated journey to Cornwall. This piece is from an illuminated, or painted, manuscript created in the late 1400s.

indicate her arrival. But Tristan's wife, jealous of Iseult, opened the letter and changed the instructions. When Iseult's ship was sighted, it was flying a black sail. Shattered by his grief, Tristan threw himself on his sword. Iseult arrived just as he gasped his last breaths. Iseult could not live without Tristan, and she died soon afterward of a broken heart.

Who is Uther Pendragon?

Uther Pendragon was ruler of England and the father of King Arthur. At Uther's coronation ceremony, he fell in love with Ygraine, the wife of Gorlois, the Duke of Cornwall. His flirtation was so obvious that Gorlois left the coronation in a rage and prepared for war against Uther. Gorlois sent Ygraine to Tintagel, a castle that was invulnerable to attack. Uther turned to his magician, Merlin, for help to get into Tintagel. Merlin had the ability to see events in the future, and he knew that Uther and Ygraine would conceive England's greatest king—Arthur. With magic spells, Merlin made Uther look like Gorlois. Thus disguised, Uther slipped into Tintagel and spent the night with Ygraine. That night, Gorlois died in a battle with Uther's army. When Arthur was born, Uther handed the baby to Merlin, who left him with the knight Sir Ector to be raised as any other child.

What is the Sword in the Stone?

After the death of King Uther, his knights argued among themselves over who should be the next king. Finally, the great wizard, Merlin, ordered the nobles and knights to gather in London. When they had all crowded into London's main cathedral, Merlin revealed a mysterious stone with a sword embedded into it. Chiseled into the stone were the words: "Whoever pulls the sword from this stone is the rightful king of all England."

Naturally, each knight and noble believed that he was the true king. Boastful and full of confidence, they took their turns straining, tugging, and pulling at the sword. But at the end of the day, their hopes were dashed. The sword did not budge. Instead, it remained in the churchyard for several years. Every year, hopefuls wrapped their hands around the sword's handle and tried their luck. But no one succeeded.

How did Arthur become King of England?

London often hosted exciting pageants and festivals full of jousts and merriment. Arthur, only a small boy, went with his foster-father, Sir Ector, and foster-brother, Kay, to the tournaments. As Kay prepared to take part in a game, he discovered that his sword was missing. Angry, he sent Arthur back to their lodgings to retrieve it. Arthur scrambled through the city streets, eager to fetch his brother's sword and return as soon as possible. But to his despair, the lodgings were locked. Suddenly, Arthur spied the sword lodged in the stone. While no one was watching, he crept up to the stone and pulled on the handle. The sword slipped out easily.

Kay immediately recognized the sword when Arthur gave it to him. Proudly, he went to his father and exclaimed that he had retrieved the sword from the stone. Shocked, Sir Ector took Arthur and Kay back to the stone and demanded to know exactly what had happened. Kay decided he could no longer lie, so he admitted to his father that Arthur had brought the sword. Nervous, Arthur explained that he had simply borrowed it. Sir Ector took the sword and stuck it back into the stone. He and Kay grabbed at it, but the sword refused to move. Arthur took the sword up again. Arthur's foster-father gasped and collapsed to his knees. He explained to Arthur that he was not his true son and that Merlin had brought Arthur to him when he was only a baby. Arthur was the true King of England.

What was Excalibur?

Although Arthur had proved himself king, many knights and barons refused to respect his rule. Arthur had to lead his army through several battles to crush his enemies and establish his power. With Merlin's aid, Arthur built a capital city at Camelot where he brought together the Knights of the Round Table. Only the bravest and strongest knights were permitted to join. They vowed to uphold the standards of truth and honor.

Still, Arthur made mistakes. When he was young, he slept with Morgaine, a powerful sorceress. Arthur did not know at the time that she was his half sister. From this incestuous union, Arthur's greatest enemy was born— Mordred.

Another time, during a heated argument with one of his own knights, Arthur drew his sword. Because Arthur had acted rashly and without cause, the sword blade shattered in his hand. In despair at the loss of his weapon, Arthur wandered into the countryside. As he walked along a lake, he saw an arm rise out of the water. Gripped in the

aucquict hip Boot oc iſannce / hp
uct ſequel H ſiſt iſta Ct (andmam

King Arthur, seated in the center of this painting with Guinevere to his right, presides over the Round Table and his knights. A French artist painted this depiction for an illuminated manuscript of the later 15th century.

hand glowed a magical sword—Excalibur. The Lady of the Lake emerged from the waters and handed the powerful weapon to Arthur. Excalibur came with a magical, intricately woven scabbard. As long as he wore the scabbard, Arthur would not bleed from any wounds.

Who was Sir Lancelot?

Sir Lancelot was the most handsome, skilled, and bravest of the Knights of the Round Table. Serving faithfully by Arthur's side, Lancelot protected his king from harm. But Lancelot had one deadly fault—he fell in love with Arthur's queen, Guinevere. The two became lovers and despite their secrecy, Arthur's other knights suspected treachery. To expose the affair, Sir Mordred and twelve knights surprised Lancelot in the queen's bedroom. Lancelot escaped and returned several days later to rescue Guinevere from her punishment. The tragic episode weakened Arthur's rule and divided the Knights of the Round Table.

Followed closely by Arthur and his army, Lancelot fled England to his native France. There, Arthur besieged Lancelot in his castle. However, Arthur was forced to return to England to confront another enemy. His son, Sir Mordred, had assembled an army and had seized Camelot for himself.

How did Arthur die?

With ranks formed and weapons drawn, Arthur's army and Mordred's army tensely confronted each other across a large field. Before the battle, Arthur and Mordred came together for one last meeting. Neither leader trusted the other, so they ordered their knights to attack immediately if anyone pulled their sword. Surrounded by a small band of knights, Arthur and Mordred held their discussion. While they spoke, a snake slithered through the grass and bit a knight on the heel. Acting on reflex, the knight pulled his sword. Both armies saw the flash of the sword. Suddenly, the ranks of knights gave a shout and advanced into battle. For the next several hours, England's greatest knights slaughtered each other, until only two were left standing. Mordred lay dead, killed by Arthur, who now staggered off the field, mortally wounded. Realizing he was about to die, Arthur ordered his remaining followers to carry him from the field. He ordered his knight Bedivere to cast Excalibur into a lake, where a hand suddenly appeared and pulled it below the surface. Arthur then was carried onto a magic boat, which disappeared to the island of Avalon. There, some people say, Arthur is healing from his wounds. Sometime in the future, when England needs him most, he will return in glory and deliver victory.

NORTH AMERICA

How did North American Indians tell their myths?

American Indians settled in North America more than 20,000 years ago, after crossing a land bridge from Asia to Alaska. They spread out across the continent and established societies of individual tribes. Each tribe developed its own mythology, with its own heroes, villains, tricksters, and stories about how they came into the world. The tribe from which the myth originated is in parentheses after the question.

How was the world created? (Iroquois)

A long time ago, a race of gods and spirits lived beneath a giant tree. Clusters of lush fruit and fragrant blossoms hung in the tree's branches. In the shade beneath the tree, the gods gathered for discussions. During one meeting, the Great Ruler told the gods that a dark and watery world full of animals existed below the roots of the tree. Great Ruler decided to send a pregnant woman down to the world to give birth to a new race of people. From below, the animals were terrified when they saw the woman descending in a blaze of light. They looked around their watery world and wondered what the woman would stand on. Beaver knew that only dirt could hold her without letting her sink into the water, but dirt

American Indian Myths by Region

The varied climates, landscapes, and wildlife of North America influenced the myths American Indians told.

Indians in the Eastern part of North America lived in dense forests scattered with lakes and rivers. Many of their myths speak of forest demons, spirits, and monsters. The Eastern Indians also believed the idea of an upper and lower world ruled by a divine being.

On the flat, grassy plains of middle America, Indians became expert buffalo hunters and lived nomadic lives after the arrival of horses (brought by Spanish explorers in the 1500s). Their traveling lifestyle influenced their beliefs. The Plains Indians' mythology emphasized the importance of personal quests to enhance their relationships with spirits.

In the Northwest, Indians lived in a relatively mild climate with access to rich supplies of food, especially salmon. These Indians developed lavish ceremonies with elaborate decorations—most famously found in massive totem poles. Each clan had a mythical animal founder.

Indians in the Southwest tended to live together in villages in a dry, hot climate. They mostly farmed for their food, and their myths often use imagery of earth as a fertile mother.

could only be found at the bottom of the sea. Turtle volunteered to carry the dirt on the back of his shell. The animals worked quickly, scooping the mud onto Turtle's back until it formed a giant mass of land. Finally, the woman landed safely on the firm soil and soon gave birth to people. Since then, all earth rides on Turtle's back. When Turtle moves, great waves rise in the ocean. When he gets restless, earthquakes shake the ground.

How was land made? (Cree)

A crafty and cunning person, called Wisagatuck, planned to capture a beaver. He dammed a stream, causing water to flood around the beaver's lodge. Wisagatuck hoped to surprise the beaver when it was forced to swim out of its home. After sitting for several hours, Wisagatuck finally spotted the beaver swimming toward him. He raised his spear and waited for the precise moment to strike. But the beaver spied Wisagatuck with his weapon, and he

Sky Woman, a 20th-century painting by artist Ernest Smith, depicts the Iroquois creation myth. Above is the land of the gods and spirits, surrounding a giant tree. Below is the watery world of earth at the beginning of time. Sky Woman, pregnant with humankind, falls to earth, where a turtle rises from the depths of the sea bearing soil for her to land on.

chanted a spell to make a muskrat bite Wisagatuck. Startled by the sharp pain from the muskrat's teeth, Wisagatuck jerked his arm, and the spear splashed harmlessly into the water.

Despite escaping injury, the beaver wanted to punish Wisagatuck for trying to kill him. The next morning, Wisagatuck dismantled his dam but was surprised to discover that the water level did not drop. Instead, it rose higher and higher. This happened because all the beavers in the world were using their magic to make the water rise. Wisagatuck quickly built a raft and invited other animals to take shelter with him. For two weeks, the water rose,

Creation Myths

This buffalo hide is painted with images of important characters in the Kiowa creation myth. The humanlike figure of Saynday, who created the world, appears in the center.

Almost every culture has creation myths—stories that explain where people came from and how the world was made. Many of these myths share similar themes, such as the splitting of the earth and sky. For example, the Chinese tell of the elements forming into the Yin and Yang, which later became heaven and earth. In Egyptian, Japanese, and many North and South American myths, the world began as a body of water.

drowning every living thing except for those on the raft. At one point, an impatient muskrat dove into the water to search for land. Sadly, there was no land to be found, and he drowned. Next, a raven flew into the air, looking for dry ground. He returned to the raft disappointed.

Desperate, Wisagatuck and a wolf chanted spells to make moss grow on their raft. The wolf ran around the outside edge of the raft, causing the moss to magically swell and expand. He circled the raft until a whole new land had been created on top of the water. But even today, water still seeps through the holes in the raft as rivers, lakes, and springs.

How were the first man and woman created? (Pima)

When the Creator finished making the world and animals, he believed something was missing. He decided to make creatures like himself, since his only companion was the tricky coyote. Using clay and water, he carefully fashioned a man, but while the Creator looked for wood to build a fire, Coyote sneaked over to the small clay figure and made some adjustments. The Creator came back and, without looking closely, slipped the clay figure into the red-hot oven to bake. After the right amount of time, the Creator pulled the figure from the oven and breathed life into it, but he then realized that the figure was no longer a man. Instead, it panted and barked and wore a coat of fur just like a coyote. Creator made this being into a dog.

Although Coyote was delighted with this creature, the Creator was not satisfied. He tried again, fashioning several men and women and putting them into the oven. As they baked, Coyote strolled over and told the Creator that they were done. The Creator rushed over, took the figures from the oven, and blew life into them. To his surprise, they were pale—he had taken them out too soon! The Creator decided that the pale people would live somewhere across the ocean. He crafted more figures and put them in the oven. This time, Coyote urged him to let them cook a little longer—but they came out too dark! As he had done with the pale people, the Creator put the dark people in a place across the ocean. His patience at an end, Creator made one last batch of people and told Coyote to keep quiet. These people emerged from the oven with the perfect color—they were not undercooked or overcooked. These people became the North American Indians.

Where did corn come from? (Penobscot)

In the time before people, a young man emerged from the sea. He was created out of wind, water, and the warmth of sunlight. The man was joined by a woman, who was created from a drop of dew that fell from a leaf. The man and woman had children, and the woman became First Mother. Their children had children, and soon people crowded the land and food grew scarce. Finally, some people went to First Mother and begged her for food. Weeping bitterly, First Mother replied that she had no food to give.

Distressed by his wife's tears, her husband asked what he could do to end her suffering. She told him that in order to help her children, he had to kill her and drag her body over the ground until only her skeleton was left. Then the area must be left alone for seven days. Shocked at this request, her husband refused. But First Mother persisted, and finally, her husband and his two sons obeyed her demand. After seven days, they returned to the field and gasped at the sight. The barren ground was now covered with plants and grass—especially corn. The hungry people ate and, as First Mother had instructed, buried some of the seeds in the ground, ensuring a crop for the next year. From then on, First Mother's husband told the people to take care of First Mother's flesh—the soil—for she had died so they could live.

Where did medicine come from? (Cherokee)

When people and animals first lived on the earth, they greeted each other and spoke together often. But when people began to kill animals for food, the animals grew angry. The bears gathered together to discuss the problem. Many of them wanted to make war on humans. Others disagreed, arguing that people had sharp knives and bows and arrows. While the bears discussed the problem among themselves, the deer also had a meeting. Being peaceful creatures, the deer rejected violence and decided to use a magic curse instead. From then on, if a hunter did not pray before killing a deer, he would be struck down with disease. The fish and reptiles held their own gathering. They plotted to haunt people who killed them with horrible dreams of serpents. The birds and insects organized together and thought of diseases to spread among people.

While the animals plotted their revenge, the plants listened with growing alarm. It didn't seem fair that humans

The Indians used bark from a willow tree to cure headaches. An active ingredient in willow bark—salicylic acid—is what makes aspirin work.

This photograph, taken before 1938, shows three Medicine Men from the Blackfeet tribe: Spotted Eagle, Chief Elk, and Bull Child, participating in the Sun Dance ritual. As "weather dancers," they blow their eagle wing bone whistles to ensure good weather during the ceremony.

be cursed for killing animals in order to eat, especially since animals killed each other for food every day. Because plants cover the earth, they were able to hear each animal's plan, and they resolved to become remedies for the maladies caused by animals. From then on, people used plants to heal their diseases and soothe their injuries.

Who is Feather-woman? (Blackfoot)

On a hot, summer night, a woman named Feather-woman slept in the cool grass outside her village. When she awoke at dawn, she watched the Morning Star rise above the horizon—a brilliant, gleaming point of light. The star's beauty made her gasp, and she quickly fell in love. Excited, she told her friends about her new love, but they only laughed and made fun of her. Later, when Feather-woman sat alone by a creek, a handsome young man appeared. He told her that he was Morning Star and that he had watched her sleeping in the grass and loved her. He asked her to become his wife. Although she was shaking with fear, Feather-woman answered yes and joined him in his home in the sky.

Feather-woman loved her new life with Morning Star and his parents, Sun and Moon. She and her husband had a son, named Poia, whom Feather-woman lovingly raised. Morning Star allowed her anything except for one thing: She could not dig up a giant turnip that grew just outside their lodge. But Feather-woman grew curious, wondering what was so special about the turnip. One day, she began scraping away the earth surrounding the turnip. Helped by two birds, she finally pulled the vegetable from the soil. It left a giant hole that peeked into a tiny world of villages and people far below. Recognizing her village, she suddenly felt homesick. Guilty and nervous, she rolled the turnip back over the hole and returned to the lodge.

Morning Star returned to the lodge very sad because he knew that his wife had disobeyed him. "You can no longer live in this world," he told her, "and you have inflicted unhappiness and death onto your people because of your disobedience." The next day, Feather-woman returned to her village with Poia, and soon after, she died from grief.

How did the Sun Dance begin? (Blackfoot)

Feather-woman's son, Poia, grew up with a large scar on his head. The other children made fun of it and made him an outcast. When Poia became a young man, he asked a medicine woman how to remove his scar. She advised him to return to the world above the sky, where his father lived. Not knowing exactly where to go, Poia traveled for days, searching for an entrance to Morning Star's world. At last, he reached the Pacific Ocean, where the sun sets at the end of each day. After three days of fasting and prayers, Poia saw a path of light from the setting sun. He walked on the path till he reached the lodge of Sun and Moon. Exhausted, he fell asleep on their doorstep. When Sun discovered him the next morning, he prepared to kill him, since no mortal ever came to his world. But his wife recognized the scar on Poia's head and realized that he was her grandson. Sun and Moon welcomed the young man into their lodge, where Sun removed Poia's scar at last. Sun also taught Poia magical spells and wisdom. As a final gift before Poia returned to his tribe, Sun taught Poia the Sun Dance. Sun told Poia

The Sun Dance

The eight-day Sun Dance was held every summer before the Plains Indians began buffalo hunting. Most tribes of the plains held their own ceremonies, including the Lakotas, Cheyennes, Blackfeet, Shoshones, and Arapahos. In the Sun Dance, an individual made pledges. For example, if an illness was cured or an injury repaired during the year, the person could do a Sun Dance as a thanksgiving offering to the gods responsible for the good fortune. With these pledges, the tribe restored good will to itself and reestablished the productive forces of nature.

that if his people danced the Sun Dance every year, their illnesses would be cured.

How did Glooskap meet his match? (Algonquin)

When the Indian warrior Glooskap walked through the world, all things bowed with respect. He had spent months fighting and defeating both animals and men in combat. Even the spirits dared not challenge his strength. When he had satisfied his quest for glory, Glooskap returned home. But his wife hardly noticed him when he strode in. She was tending to something on the floor, something he had never seen before. Glooskap asked his wife what it was. She answered that it was the Wasis—a fierce creature that held both the past and future in its power. Glooskap could not believe it. After conquering the world, an enemy controlled his own home! Glooskap rushed over to the Wasis and challenged it to a contest of strength, but the Wasis ignored him. Glooskap screamed at the Wasis, telling it that he was the most powerful thing in the world. This time, the Wasis did respond. It began wailing and howling, so loud that Glooskap clapped his hands over his ears. The Wasis kept screaming. Desperate, Glooskap danced and sang songs until the Wasis stopped screaming. When the Wasis suddenly smiled and said "goo," Glooskap collapsed in exhaustion, defeated by the mighty Wasis. The Wasis, of course, is a baby, and to this day, whenever a baby smiles and says "goo," it is remembering its victory over Glooskap, ruler of man and beast.

How did Deer get his horns? (Cherokee)

Originally, Deer had a smooth head with no horns. One day, the animals decided to have a contest between Rabbit and Deer to determine who was the fastest. They would race through a dense thicket and back again, and the victor would win a magnificent pair of antlers.

On the day of the race, Rabbit asked if he could look over the course before the contest began. Everyone agreed, and Rabbit disappeared into the thicket. Alone, the cunning Rabbit began hacking a trail through the tangle of bushes and tree limbs with his teeth. But when he was almost finished, the other animals discovered his trickery. To punish Rabbit for attempting to deceive them, the other animals awarded the antlers to Deer, who still lifts them proudly. Because Rabbit seemed so good at eating bushes, the animals awarded him that task forever. To this day, Rabbit still gnaws at thickets.

MESOAMERICA

Who were the Mayans?

The Mayans were a Native American people whose culture flourished in Central America and Mexico from A.D. 300 to 900. They developed a sophisticated society with complex cities, writing, and a precise calendar. From A.D. 900 to 1200, the Mayan culture mysteriously declined so that when Spanish explorers arrived in the 1500s, they discovered several abandoned Mayan cities and magnificent works of art.

What is the Mayan myth of creation?

In the beginning, the world was a pool of motionless water beneath the sky. Within the water, Gucumatz, a serpent covered in blue and green feathers, suddenly stirred. He swam to the surface and spoke to the Heart of Heaven, a god in the sky. They discussed creation, and as they spoke, their words became real. Around them, mountains and land appeared, trees and flowers burst into bloom. Animals scampered through the forests.

How did Gucumatz and the Heart of Heaven try to create humans?

Gucumatz and the Heart of Heaven now listened for praise and prayers from their new creations, but they were disappointed. The animals couldn't speak the creators' language. Instead, they squeaked, barked, chirped, roared, and hissed, creating such a racket that the creators understood nothing. Clearly, the animals could not worship the gods properly, so the two creators decided to make people.

First, they fashioned a man and woman out of clay. They could speak, but their words were garbled, and their clay bodies melted and dissolved. Following this failure, Gucumatz and the Heart of Heaven consulted two other gods, who advised them to make their next people out of wood. But the wooden creatures were bloodless, displayed no emotion, and did not respect the gods. Disgusted, Gucumatz and the Heart of Heaven sent demons to tear them to pieces and a flood to drown whoever survived. The descendants of the wooden people were allowed to survive as monkeys, a warning to those who disrespected the gods.

How were people finally created?

Gucumatz and the Heart of Heaven called on Fox, Coyote, Parrot, and Crow to bring them yellow and white corn seeds. They ground the corn into a paste and fashioned the first four men. At first, Gucumatz and the Heart of Heaven were thrilled with their new creations. The four men were intelligent and quickly gave proper thanks and praise to their creators. But soon, Gucumatz and the Heart of Heaven realized that the men were too smart, and that they had the ability to see into heaven itself. Deciding that the four men were too much like gods, Gucumatz and the Heart of Heaven blurred their vision, so they could only see what was around them. Gucumatz and the Heart of Heaven also gave the four men gifts of happiness—four beautiful wives as companions. These four couples reproduced and filled the world with people.

Who were the Aztecs?

The Aztecs created a magnificent empire that covered most of Mexico from the 1300s to 1521. They constructed

The Aztec Empire has had a tremendous influence on Mexican culture. Today, more than one million Mexicans still speak Nahuatl, the Aztec language, and many places in Mexico retain their original Aztec name, such as Popocatepetl and Mt. Iztaccihuatl.

their capital city, Tenochtitlan, upon land reclaimed from a lake and marshes. Among its many buildings were spectacular pyramids. When Tenochtitlan was conquered by the Spanish in 1521, it may have been the largest city in the world.

What are the four Aztec suns?

The Aztecs believed that four worlds or eras, called suns, existed before their own. In the first sun, powerful giants roamed the earth. But the two gods, Quetzalcoatl and Tezcatlipoca, quarreled and began fighting. Quetzalcoatl hit Tezcatlipoca with his staff, sending him tumbling into the ocean. Tezcatlipoca reemerged as a giant jaguar, and he began feasting on the giants until they were all consumed.

In this carving, the god Quetzalcoatl is depicted as a coiled serpent covered with feathers, its tongue drooping out of its half-opened mouth. This stone carving was created by Aztec craftsmen in the 1400s.

The Aztec Gods

The Aztec gods and people descended from the great creator god, Ometecuhtli.

Quetzalcoatl is the offspring of Ometecuhtli. He is represented as a serpent decorated with beautiful feathers. The Aztecs believed that Quetzalcoatl was a kind god who brought rain clouds and nurtured crops.

Tezcatlipoca, the god of night and sorcery, brought chaos and destruction. A mysterious god, he is often portrayed with a smoky mirror at his head and feet, in which he could see the future and determine the thoughts of men. In Nahuatl, his name means "Lord of the Smoking Mirror."

Tlaloc is the god of lightning and rain. He is associated with mountain tops, where clouds and mists gathered and rivers originated.

Chalchiuhtlicue is Tlaloc's companion. She is the goddess of rivers and pools of water.

Centeotl is the god of corn, or maize.

Xipe Totec is the god of spring and the inspiration of craftsmen who work with gold.

Xochipilli is called the Flower Prince. He is the god of pleasure and the arts. Xochiquetzal is the beautiful goddess of arts and love. She is the twin sister of Xochipilli and wears a headband decorated with flowers.

The god Mictlantecuhtli ruled Mictlan, the gloomy underworld. He is often portrayed as a skeleton.

Tonatiuh is god of the sun.

In the second sun, Quetzalcoatl created a race of people, but Tezcatlipoca attacked him and brought fierce blasts of wind to sweep the people away. The survivors changed as they adapted to their surroundings and became monkeys in the forest.

In the third sun, Quetzalcoatl created a massive volcanic explosion that destroyed almost everything in a rain of fire. The people were changed into birds and butterflies.

In the fourth sun, a giant flood washed away the mountains and brought the heavens crashing down to earth. This world's people were changed into fish. One man and one woman, however, survived by floating in a hollow tree trunk. They survived on corn they had saved until the water had dried up. When they stepped onto land, they caught some fish and built a fire to cook them. But the drifting smoke irritated the gods in heaven. In a

Tezcatlipoca, one of the most powerful gods of the Aztecs, stands on the water and tempts a monster to the surface by offering his foot as bait. This style of illustration was often used in codexes, or painted records of pre-European Central American society and culture.

fury, Tezcatlipoca came down to earth and cut off their heads and lay them on their rear ends. Thus, dogs were created.

How was the world created?

Another Aztec myth describes the earth goddess, Tlaltecuhtli, as a fierce beast with several gaping mouths full of teeth. Quetzalcoatl and Tezcatlipoca watched Tlaltecuhtli as she crossed the ocean, her hungry mouths searching for food. Repulsed by the disgusting monster, Quetzalcoatl and Tezcatlipoca decided to destroy her. Transforming themselves into giant serpents, they descended from heaven and attacked Tlaltecuhtli. Quetzalcoatl siezed one foot, Tezcatlipoca grabbed the other, and they pulled in opposite directions, tearing the monster in two. Quetzalcoatl and Tezcatlipoca took one half of the body and created the earth. They threw the other half into the sky, creating the heavens.

Human Sacrifice

Human sacrifice was an important ritual in Aztec religion. The gods had given their own blood to create mankind, and the Aztecs believed that they wanted human flesh and blood as sacrifice. The Aztecs also believed that human blood contained *chalchihuatl*, a liquid the gods needed for nourishment. Most often, prisoners of war were used for the ritual. According to legend, Aztec priests sacrificed eighty thousand prisoners of war in one year to the Aztec sun god Toniatuh.

The strands of Tlaltecuhtli's hair became flowers, herbs, and the trees of the forest. Her skin became rolling fields of grass. Her eyes were formed into wells, springs, and small caves. Her mouths were the source of rivers, and her nose formed mountain ridges and valleys.

To give people the fruit and grains they needed for life, Tlaltecuhtli demanded a bloody payment made with human hearts. It became an important Aztec ritual to sacrifice people to Tlaltecuhtli to ensure that she continued to yield life-giving food.

How were people made?

With the world created, the gods decided to make people. The other gods ordered Quetzalcoatl to journey to the underworld, Mictlan, and retrieve the bones of people who were turned into fish. But Mictlan was ruled by the crafty Mictlantecuhtli, who promised the bones to Quetzalcoatl, but only if he could complete one task. He asked Quetzalcoatl to take a shell and blow it in four separate spots in Mictlan. Quetzalcoatl took the shell, but Mictlantecuhtli gave him one without holes to blow in. Quetzalcoatl ordered worms to eat holes and bees to fly into the shell and create a loud blast. Having completed the task, Quetzalcoatl took the bones and fled. But Mictlantecuhtli tried one last time to stop him. He ordered his followers to dig a huge pit. When Quetzalcoatl ran up the path, a small bird flew into his face and tripped him into the pit. The bones scattered from his grasp, some breaking in the fall. For this reason, people are of different sizes—some tall and others short. Quetzalcoatl jumped from the pit and escaped Mictlan at last. When Quetzalcoatl returned to the other gods, an old goddess took the bones and ground them into a fine powder. The other gods gathered around, adding their own blood into the mixture to create the first humans.

Where did corn come from?

After the gods created people, they searched for suitable food to keep them alive. One day, Quetzalcoatl noticed a tiny red ant carrying a grain of corn and asked him where he found it. The ant refused to tell him, so Quetzalcoatl changed himself into a black ant and followed the red ant to his home. The red ant led Quetzalcoatl deep below a mountain into a maze of tunnels and rooms where Quetzalcoatl found giant storerooms filled with grain and corn. He took some of the corn and returned to the other gods, who were amazed at his find. They took the corn, mashed it, and then fed it to the human babies. It was perfect, but they didn't know how to get more. Quetzalcoatl returned to the mountain and tried to carry it off with a rope, but it was too heavy. Then another god, Nanahuatzin, used lightning and rain to split the mountain open, scattering the grains throughout the world. The gods snatched up the grains of corn and beans, as well as other valuable seeds, and gave them to the Aztec people.

How were the sun and the moon created?

Even after people and food were created, darkness still shrouded the world, and the gods discussed how they could provide light to the earth. One god, Tecuciztecatl, arrogantly volunteered to become the sun. The other gods elected Nanahuatzin, a humble god who was crippled with disease. Finally, the gods decided they would have a contest to see who would become the sun.

First, both gods did penance and purified themselves through sacrifices. Tecuciztecatl offered rare gifts of magnificent quality and beauty. Nanahuatzin could only give cheap, common items. Tecuciztecatl dressed himself in lovely robes. Nanahuatzin wore simple clothing made from paper.

After four days of sacrifice, a giant pyre was prepared. Both gods had to rush into the flames and whoever was

The leering god of death, Mictlantecuhtli, ruled over the gloomy underworld. This clay pottery figure shows him as a skeleton because myths told the story that on their way to the underworld, the dead were stripped of their flesh by a wind of knives.

purest would emerge as the sun. Tecuciztecatl ran toward the leaping bonfire, but the flames and heat terrified him and he suddenly stopped. Humiliated, he backed up and tried again. He failed again. The gods grew impatient and told Nanahuatzin to take his turn. Without pause, Nanahuatzin raced and jumped into the searing heat. Shamed, Tecuciztecatl followed him. Both gods were immediately consumed in the blaze.

The other gods waited eagerly for the dawn to see who would emerge as the sun. Gradually, the sky grew light, and a disc of blinding light appeared on the horizon. It was Nanahuatzin. He no longer suffered illness as he blazed in the sky. But then another disc appeared on the horizon just as bright as Nanahuatzin. It was Tecuciztecatl. The gods suddenly worried that now there would be too much light.

One of the gods strode forward and threw a rabbit in front of Tecuciztecatl, dimming his brilliance. Thus, Tecuciztecatl became the moon, a lesser light than the sun. Today, if you look closely at a full moon, you might be able to see the rabbit's face.

Who was Tonatiuh?

As the sun, Nanahuatzin became Tonatiuh. Proud of his new power, Tonatiuh hung in the sky and refused to move unless the gods provided sacrifice with their own blood. The Lord of the Dawn, angered by Tonatiuh's demand, threw a dart at him. But the dart sailed wide, and the sun fired back, hitting the Lord of the Dawn in the head and making him cold. For this reason, the dawn is always chilly.

The other gods realized that resistance was useless, and they cut out their own hearts as a sacrifice to Tonatiuh. Later, the Aztecs would keep this tradition by tearing out the hearts of human sacrifices in order to please Tonatiuh and keep the sun moving across the sky.

How was Tenochtitlan founded?

Long before the Aztec people founded their great empire, they lived in a community of many tribes in a place called Chicomoztoc (Seven Caves). But the people grew restless and tribes began to leave. The Aztecs were the last to go. One of their gods, Huitzilopochtli, which means Hummingbird of the South, put visions into the heads of the Aztec priests, telling them where they should go. They traveled far and long. In some places, the people settled and were reluctant to move on. But Huitzilopochtli grew angry when this happened, and he sent visions urging the people to move on.

Some among the Aztecs quarreled, leaving the tribe divided. One troublemaker, named Macuilxochitl, or Wild Grass Flower, grew so powerful and evil that many Aztecs begged their priests to abandon her. One morning, the rest of the tribe slipped out of camp in silence, leaving Macuilxochitl behind. When she awoke, she swore revenge and sent her son, Copil, to spread trouble for the Aztecs.

Copil traveled to other villages and warned them that the Aztecs were an evil people who wanted to conquer

Myth and Tragic Reality

The two gods—Quetzalcoatl and Tezcatlipoca—constantly battled to determine who would rule the universe. After one fight, Quetzalcoatl was driven from his capital city, Tenochtitlan, by Tezcatlipoca. According to Aztec myth, Quetzalcoatl would eventually return in triumph as a light-skinned, bearded god. In 1519, the Aztec king, Moctezuma II was shocked when a light-skinned, bearded Spaniard named Hernán Cortés arrived in the capital city. Moctezuma was convinced that Quetzalcoatl had returned at last. But Moctezuma was very wrong. Cortés was not a god, but a conquistador in search of gold and riches. With Indian allies and European guns, Cortés and his men destroyed the Aztec Empire in 1521.

them. Soon, the Aztecs discovered angry enemies wherever they went. Huitzilopochtli warned his people and instructed the Aztec warriors to surprise Copil in a cave where he was hiding and kill him. They tore his heart from his chest and, as ordered by Huitzilopochtli, cast it into a Lake Texcoco.

The Aztecs continued to dwell among enemies, and they constantly had to fight battles and move on. It seemed that their wanderings would never end.

Finally, Huitzilopochtli appeared in the priests' dreams and told them where they were to create their empire. He told them that a prickly pear cactus seed had taken root in Copil's heart. The cactus had grown tall, and an eagle had built a nest among its needles. The god told the Aztecs to look for the eagle with its wings outstretched, perched on a cactus that grew on a rock. There, he said, you will found a city named Tenochtitlan.

The Aztecs did as the Huitzilopochtli had ordered. They found the cactus tree with the eagle in its top branches. There they founded their capital city and called it Tenochtitlan, which means place of the prickly pear cactus. This brought their long and difficult wanderings to an end.

The Mexican flag still bears the emblem of an eagle with a snake in its mouth, perched on a cactus growing out of a rock.

GLOSSARY

A

Aesir the race of Norse gods led by Odin

afterlife the soul's existence after the death of the body

Amazon a member of the tribe of courageous female warriors in Greek myths

armada a fleet of warships

artifact something that is created by human hands, especially primitive art, weapons, and tools

Asgard home to the Norse gods the Aesir

B

Banshee a Celtic spirit whose wailing cries told of imminent death

brahman a Hindu priest

C

Cerberes the three-headed dog who guarded the entrance to the underworld in Greek mythology

chaos a condition without order or laws. Creation myths usually begin by describing a period of chaos before the orderly universe was created

Charybdis a monster whirlpool that sucked in and devoured anything that came near. In Greek mythology, Odysseus encounters Charybdis off the coast of Sicily

chariot an ancient two-wheeled cart drawn by horses. Chariots were used in races and battle

codex an ancient painted record, usually of early Central American culture

Cornwall a county in southwest England

Creation myth the story in a mythology that explains how the world and humans came into being

Cyclops a one-eyed giant; their eye was believed to be in the center of their forehead

D

demigod/demigoddess a being that is stronger than a mortal but not as strong as a god

dragon a mythical fierce creature that is usually like a serpent, although it can be a combination of creatures. Dragons were often depicted as breathing fire in medieval times

dwarf a short, humanlike creature that lived beneath the earth in Norse mythology and created stunning works of craftsmanship

E

embroider to adorn cloth or fabric with needlework patterns

F

fairy a mythical spirit, usually in the form of a tiny human, that interferes with peoples' lives for good and evil

Fianna the fierce band of warriors who protected the king of Ireland

Firbolg a legendary race of Irish people

Formorians an evil race of giants who, according to Celtic mythology, inhabited Ireland

G

Gorgon one of three female monsters in Greek mythology who were covered with dragon scales and had snakes for hair. The Gorgons turned people to stone with their hideous gaze

Graeae three old witches in Greek mythology who shared one eye and one tooth between them

H

Han dynasty Chinese imperial dynasty dating from 207 B.C. to 220 A.D. China was reunited during the Han dynasty, which is considered a golden age of Chinese philosophy and learning

homage a tribute paid to show respect to another person or god

Hydra a huge snake with nine heads; one of the monsters defeated by Herakles

I

immortality life without end

invincible impossible to conquer

J

Jigoku a world where sinful people go after they die. According to Japanese mythology, Jigoku has eight realms of fire and eight realms of ice. Souls must stand before a mirror that reflects their sins

K

kami the spirits and gods of the Shinto religion

M

mango a sweet tropical fruit

marrow fatty tissue inside bones

mead an alcoholic beverage made from honey

Mictlan the Aztec underworld

Midgard Serpent a giant snake that encircled the entire world according to Norse mythology

Minotaur a monster that was half man and half bull. According to Greek mythology, the Minotaur lived in a labyrinth on the island of Crete and ate human sacrifices

Mount Olympus a mountain in Greece; the mythical home of the twelve Olympian gods

Muse any of the nine Greek goddesses that inspired the arts and sciences

muskrat an aquatic rodent with brown fur, webbed feet, and a scaly tail

N

Nidhogg a dragon who lived in the Norse underworld. Nidhogg ate human corpses and gnawed at the roots of Yggdrasill

Niflheim the dark, frozen, foggy underworld in Norse mythology

nomad a member of a people with no fixed homes who move from place to place in search of food or according to the seasons

Norns three beings in Norse mythology who watered the roots of the tree Yggdrasill and decided people's fate. The three Norns were Urd (Fate), Verdandi (the Present), and Skuld (the Future)

Norse Scandinavian

nymphs creatures in classical mythology who are represented as beautiful maidens or young girls living in forests, mountains, trees, or water

O

odyssey a long and dangerous voyage. The word comes from the name of the Greek hero, Odysseus, who wandered twenty years before he could come home

Olympian one of the twelve gods that defeated the Titans and ruled the universe in Greek mythology

omniscience the quality of having universal and infinite knowledge

Oni evil demon spirits that the Japanese believed brought misery and illness into the world

oracle a shrine where a god reveals divine knowledge or information about the future

P

pedestal the base of a column

penance self-imposed suffering that purifies a soul of sin

portal a doorway or entrance

primeval mound the first ground to appear in creation. Many mythologies begin their creation stories with the appearance of the primeval mound

pyramid massive stone structure with a square base and four triangular sides that meet in a point at the top. The most famous pyramids were those erected by the ancient Egyptians as tombs for the pharoahs. Most of the largest Egyptian pyramids were built around 2600 B.C.

pyre the pile of material used for a fire or the fire of a funeral pyre

python a large snake

R

Ragnarok in Norse mythology, the final battle in which all the gods and humans are destroyed

relief a type of sculpture where the forms and figures are raised from the background

S

saga a long narrative, often composed of many stories, that recounts heroic deeds

sake Japanese rice wine

satyr a creature in Greek mythology who was half man and half goat

Scandinavia region in northern Europe made up of Norway, Sweden, Denmark, and Iceland

Scylla a six-headed monster who lived in a cave on one side of a narrow strait and devoured any prey that came near

She-wolf female wolf

Shinto a Japanese religion that has been important in Japan since prehistoric times. In its early period, Shinto did not have strict beliefs or sacred texts. Shinto faded in importance but was revived in the eighteenth century. Until the end of World War II, the Shinto worshipped the Emperor as a descendant of Amaterasu, the Sun goddess

silk a soft, fine thread produced by silkworms. Silk clothing is generally regarded as very luxurious

siren a creature with the head of a woman and the body of a bird. In Greek mythology, sirens sang beautiful songs and lured sailors to their deaths

Sleipnir Odin's eight-legged horse

sphinx a creature in Greek mythology with the head and chest of a woman, the body of a lion, and the wings of a bird. Sphinx outside Thebes killed travelers who were unable to answer her riddle. In Egyptian mythology, a sphinx could have the head of a man, a ram, or a hawk

Sub-Saharan referring to the region of Africa located south of the Sahara Desert

T

Tenochtitlan the capital city of the Aztec empire, located in what is now Mexico City

Titan one of twelve powerful creatures in Greek mythology. The six male Titans and the six female Titanesses were the children of Gaea (Mother Earth) and Uranus (the Heavens)

totem pole a pillar carved and painted with symbols representing mythological or historical events or family history. Native Americans of the Northwest often fashioned totem poles

trickster a character that relies on guile and cunning, rather than brute strength, to overcome odds and get what they want

trident a three-pronged spear. The sea god (Poseidon in Greek mythology and Neptune in Roman mythology) carried a powerful trident

Tuatha Dé Danann the race of Celtic gods

U

underworld a place in most mythologies where the spirits of the dead dwell

Utgard a fortress built by the frost giants in Norse mythology

V

Valhalla an enormous hall that housed the Norse warriors who died heroically in battle. The slain heroes battled during the day and had great feasts at night

Valkyrie a warrior demigoddess in Norse mythology

Vanaheim home of the Norse gods the Vanir

Vanir an elder race of Norse gods who fought with the Aesir for control of the world.

Vedic gods early Indian gods who usually represented the primal forces of fire, wind, and rain

Viking a race of Norsemen who plundered the coasts of Europe from the eighth to the eleventh centuries

Y

yang the male principle in Chinese belief that represents light, heat, and dryness. Together with the yin, the yang symbolizes the balance of opposite features that form the universe, such as good and evil or day and night

Yggdrasill a gigantic tree in the center of the universe. According to Norse mythology, Yggdrasill's branches supported nine separate worlds

yin the female principle in Chinese belief that represents darkness, cold and wetness. Togther with the yang, the yin symbolizes the opposite features that come together to form the universe, such as dark and light or female and male

Yomi the dark world where the spirits of the dead live in Japanese mythology

SELECTED BIBLIOGRAPHY

Bennett, Martin. *West African Trickster Tales*. Oxford: Oxford University Press, 1994.

Bierhorst, John. *The Mythology of Mexico and Central America*. New York: William Morrow, 1990.

Bierlein, J. F. *Parallel Myths*. New York: Ballantine Books, 1994.

Birrell, Anne. *Chinese Mythology*. Baltimore and London: The Johns Hopkins University Press, 1993.

Campbell, Joseph. *Occidental Mythology*. New York: Viking Penguin Inc., 1964.

————, *Oriental Mythology*. New York: Viking Penguin Inc., 1962.

Carpenter, Thomas H. *Art and Myth in Ancient Greece*. London: Thames and Hudson, 1991.

Cotterell, Arthur. *The Encyclopedia of Mythology*. London: Anness Publishing Limited, 1996.

Courlander, Harold. *A Treasury of African Folklore*. New York: Crown Publishers, Inc., 1975.

Dalley, Stephen. *Myths from Mesopotamia*. Oxford: Oxford University Press, 1989.

Davidson, H. R. Ellis. *Gods and Myths of Northern Europe*. London: Penguin Books, 1964.

Erdoes, Richard and Alfonso Ortiz. *American Indian Myths and Legends*. New York: Pantheon Books, 1984.

Fagles, Robert, ed. *The Iliad*. New York: Penguin Books USA, Inc., 1990.

————, ed. *The Odyssey.* New York: Penguin Books USA, Inc., 1997.

————, ed. *Sophocles: The Three Theban Plays: Antigone, Oedipus the King, Oedipus at Colonus.* New York: Penguin Books, 1984.

Gantz, Jeffrey. *Early Irish Myths and Sagas.* London: Penguin Books, 1981.

Gardner, Jane F. *Roman Myths.* London: British Museum Press, 1993.

Goodrich, Norma Lorre. *The Ancient Myths.* New York: Mentor Books, 1960.

Green, Miranda Jane. *Celtic Myths.* London: British Museum Press, 1993.

Hamilton, Edith. *Mythology.* Boston: Little, Brown & Company, 1940.

Hart, George. *Egyptian Myths.* London: British Museum Press, 1990.

Hendricks, Rhoda A. *Classical Gods and Heroes.* New York: Morrow Quill Paperbacks, 1974.

Jordan, Michael. *Eastern Wisdom.* New York: Marlowe & Company, n.d.

Lattimore, Richmond, ed. *Aeschylus I: Oresteia.* Chicago: The University of Chicago Press, 1953.

————, ed. *The Iliad of Homer.* Chicago: The University of Chicago Press, 1951.

Leeming, David Adams. *The World of Myth.* New York: Oxford University Press, 1990.

Mandlebaum, Allen, ed. *The Aeneid of Virgil.* New York: Bantam Books, 1971.

————, ed. *The Metamorphoses of Ovid.* New York: Harcourt Brace, 1993.

Miller, Barbara Stoller. *The Bhagavad-Gita: Krishna's Counsel in Time of War.* New York: Bantam Classics, 1986.

Narayan, R. K. *The Ramayana: A Shortened Modern Prose Version of the Indian Epic.* New York: Penguin USA, 1993.

Page, R. I. *Norse Myths.* London: British Museum Press, 1990.

Pabhavananda, Swami and Christopher Isherwood, eds. *The Bhagavad Gita: The Song of God.* New York: Mentor Books, 1954.

Philip, Neil. *The Illustrated Book of Myths.* London: Dorling Kindersley Limited, 1995.

————. *Odin's Family: Myths of the Vikings.* New York: Orchard Books, 1996.

Piggott, Juliet. *Japanese Mythology*. Middlesex: The Hamlyn Publishing Group Limited, 1969.

Reed, Alexander Wyclif. *Aboriginal Stories*. Chatswood: Reed Books, 1994.

Rosenberg, Donna. *World Mythology: An Anthology of Great Myths and Epics*. Lincolnwood, Illinois: Passport Books, 1992.

Sandars, N.K., ed. *The Epic of Gilgamesh: An English Version with an Introduction*. New York: Penguin USA, 1987.

Savory, Phyllis. *The Best of African Folklore*. Cape Town: Struik Timmins Publishers, 1988.

Switzer, Ellen. *Greek Myths: Gods, Heroes and Monsters*. New York: Atheneum, 1988.

Taube, Karl. *Aztec and Maya Myths*. London: British Museum Press, 1993.

Turner, Frederick, ed. *The Portable North American Indian Reader*. New York: The Viking Press, 1973.

Wender, Dorothea, ed. *Hesiod: Theogony, Works and Days; Theognis: Elegies*. New York, Penguin Books, 1973.

Willis, Roy, ed. *Mythology: An Illustrated Guide*. London: Duncan Baird Publishers, 1998.

Young, Jean I., ed. *The Prose Edda of Snorri Sturlson: Tales from Norse Mythology*. Berkeley, California: University of California Press, 1964.

THE NEW YORK PUBLIC LIBRARY'S
RECOMMENDED READING LIST

Bierlein, J. F. *Parallel Myths*. New York: Ballantine Books, 1994.

Bulfinch, Thomas. *Bulfinch's Mythology*. New York: Modern Library, 1998.

Goodrich, Norma Lorre. *The Ancient Myths*. New York: Mentor Books, 1960.

Graves, Robert. *The Greek Myths*. New York: Penguin USA, 1993.

Hamilton, Edith. *Mythology*. Boston: Little, Brown & Company, 1940.

Hamilton, Virginia. *In the Beginning: Creation Stories From Around the World*. San Diego: Harcourt Brace Jovanovich, 1988.

Harris, Geraldine. *Gods & Pharaohs from Egyptian Mythology*. New York: P. Bedrick Books, 1981.

Hendricks, Rhoda A. *Classical Gods and Heroes*. New York: Morrow Quill Paperbacks, 1974.

Husain, Shahrukh. *Demons, Gods & Holy Men from Indian Myths and Legends*. New York: P. Bedrick Books, 1987.

Oodgeroo. *Dreamtime: Aboriginal Stories*. New York: Lothrop Lee & Shepard, 1994.

Philip, Neil. *The Illustrated Book of Myths*. London: Dorling Kindersley Limited, 1995.

Philip, Neil. *Odin's Family: Myths of the Vikings*. New York: Orchard Books, 1996.

Ross, Anne. *Druids, Gods & Heroes From Celtic Mythology*. New York: P. Bedrick Books, 1986.

Sanders, Tao Tao Liu. *Dragons, Gods & Spirits From Chinese Mythology*. New York: P. Bedrick Books, 1980.

Turner, Frederick, ed. *The Portable North American Indian Reader.* New York: The Viking Press, 1973.

Waldher, Kris. *The Book of Goddesses.* Hillsboro, Oregon: Beyond Words, 1995.

Zimmerman, John Edward. *Dictionary of Classical Mythology.* Bantam Books, 1983.

INDEX

Note: Page numbers in italics indicate illustrations.

PHOTOGRAPHY CREDITS